THE

RIGHT TO

PRIVACY

edited by GRANT S. McCLELLAN

Editor, *Current Magazine*

THE REFERENCE SHELF
Volume 48   Number 1

THE H. W. WILSON COMPANY

New York   1976

THE REFERENCE SHELF

The books in this series contain reprints of articles, excerpts from books, and addresses on current issues and social trends in the United States and other countries. There are six separately bound numbers in each volume, all of which are generally published in the same calendar year. One number is a collection of recent speeches; each of the others is devoted to a single subject and gives background information and discussion from various points of view, concluding with a comprehensive bibliography. Books in the series may be purchased individually or on subscription.

Library of Congress Cataloging in Publication Data
Main entry under title:

The Right to privacy.

(The Reference shelf ; v. 48, no. 1)
Bibliography: p.
1. Privacy, Right of—United States—Addresses, essays, lectures.   I. McClellan, Grant S.
II. Series.
KF1262.A75R52   342'.73'085   75-45252
ISBN 0-8242-0595-2

PREFACE

Why the recent intensifying interest in the right to privacy in America? This question is succinctly answered in this compilation by Constance Holden of *Science* magazine:

Over the years, legal scholars have attempted to define privacy —one of the earliest is Louis D. Brandeis's formulation of it in 1890 as "the right to be let alone." A later formulation by Alan F. Westin of Columbia University is that privacy is "the claim of individuals, groups or institutions to determine for themselves when, how and to what extent information about themselves is communicated to others." Privacy is not defined by the Constitution although the preponderance of legal opinion has it that the right to privacy is implicit in the Bill of Rights.

Holden proceeds to point out that privacy cannot be strictly defined. Consequently Congress has chosen to establish procedures enabling individuals to take measures to protect whatever they perceive to be their privacy. The 1974 Privacy Act is the first federal statute to establish this right.

The Bureau of the Budget's proposal to set up a centralized, automated National Data Bank pooling the files of the Internal Revenue Service, the Social Security Administration, and the Census Bureau roused a storm of protest. The proposal was quashed. As citizens found themselves increasingly numbered and coded, the public became increasingly conscious of the possibility of a computer takeover. Watergate increased the sense of urgency and a new Committee on the Right of Privacy was set up within the White House Domestic Council. Under the supervision of Douglas Metz, a former management consultant executive, the committee has worked well with Congress and given the issue high-level visibility and support.

Furthermore, in Congress itself, a coalition of conservatives and civil libertarians (two usually divergent factions)

3

has boosted privacy proposals into law. In the Senate former Senator Sam Ervin (Democrat, North Carolina) and Senator Roman Hruska (Republican, Nebraska) joined forces; liberal Edward Koch (Democrat, New York) and conservative Barry Goldwater Jr. (Republican, California) were allied in the House.

The growth of interest detailed here regarding the right to privacy can be seen to be extensive—citizen concern about the "heedless army of computers" with dossiers on individuals across the nation, and intensive congressional and top-level federal government action. It is in these areas that information has been amassed and analyses made. It must be noted that for reasons of space and lack of significant overall coverage, material on the problems and the action (or lack of it) at state and local levels is not included here.

In Section I of this compilation some of the broad, philosophic questions of privacy are explored. Section II discusses federal government concern (or indifference). Topics covered range from applications of new technology to criminal justice procedures through government information systems and the scope of electronic surveillance, to the National Security Agency. The spate of recent revelations concerning invasions of privacy by the Federal Bureau of Investigation and the Central Intelligence Agency is dealt with in Section III.

Surveyed in Section IV are problems arising from infringement of citizens' rights by computerized banking systems, two-way cable TV, the spread of medical information systems, and the release of student records. The section ends with a consideration of the right of privacy versus the rights of a free press.

In Section V an examination of the landmark national Privacy Act of 1974 is followed by reports on implementation of the act and articles looking toward future efforts to insure greater privacy.

The editor wishes to thank the authors and publishers of

the selections which follow for permission to reprint them in this compilation.

GRANT S. McCLELLAN

January 1976

NOTE TO THE READER

The reader's attention is directed to Section II, The Watergate Scandal, of an earlier Reference Shelf compilation, *The President and the Constitution* (Volume 46, Number 4), edited by George A. Nikolaieff and published in 1974.

CONTENTS

PREFACE 3

I. PRIVACY IN A FREE SOCIETY

Editor's Introduction 11
Aryeh Neier .... Privacy, Society, and Dossiers 12
Marguerite Guzman Bouvard and Jacques Bouvard.
    Computers and Individual Rights .... Society 25
Arthur S. Miller. Do Americans Value Privacy? ......
    .... Privacy Report 40
Barbara L. Kaiser. Privacy Is Not Solitude ....
    .... Privacy Report 43
Stephen Arons. The Rise of Police Logic ....
    .... Saturday Review 45
Thomas J. Cottle. Is Privacy Possible? ....
    .... New Republic 53

II. GOVERNMENT AND PRIVACY

Editor's Introduction 63
Mark H. Gitenstein. The New Technology of Criminal
    Justice Administration .... Trial 64
Clarence M. Kelley. Criminal Justice Information Sys-
    tems .... Trial 75
Nicholas M. Horrock. The Scope of Electronic Surveil-
    lance .... New York Times 81
Robert Ellis Smith. The Wired Nation: Wiretaps ....
    .... Privacy Journal 86
Snooping Into Tax Returns ....
    .... U.S. News & World Report 90

Morton H. Halperin. The National Security Agency
    and Domestic Spying .... New Republic 95
Police Search Without Warrant:
    1. Frank Carrington. An Argument in Favor ....
       .... Christian Science Monitor 101
    2. Lloyd L. Weinreb. An Opposing Viewpoint ....
       .... Christian Science Monitor 103

III.   THE ROLE OF THE FBI AND THE CIA

Editor's Introduction 106
John M. Crewdson. An FBI Case History ....
    .... New York Times 106
Richard L. Strout. The Rockefeller CIA Report ......
    .... Christian Science Monitor 110
Frank J. Donner. Investigating Intelligence Agencies ..
    .... Nation 117
Irving Louis Horowitz. Dealing With the CIA and the
    FBI .... Society 127
Arthur Schlesinger, Jr. How to Control the CIA ....
    .... Wall Street Journal 134
John Ligonier, pseud. A Favorable Word for the CIA
    .... Human Events 140

IV.   INDIVIDUAL PRIVACY CASES

Editor's Introduction 147
Dori Jones. Social Security Numbers and Privacy ....
    .... National Observer 148
Paul Armer. Computerized Banking ....
    .... Privacy Journal 152
Jerrold Oppenheim. Cable TV and Privacy ....
    .... Cable Report 156
Natalie Davis Spingarn. Privacy and Medical Practice
    .... Washington Post 161

Trudy R. Hayden. Student Privacy Rights . . . .
. . . . Privacy Report 175
Martin Arnold. Privacy Versus the Press . . . .
. . . . New York Times 187
Alan L. Otten. Privacy of Presidents . . . .
. . . . Wall Street Journal 191
W. H. Hornby. On Balancing Rights . . . .
. . . . Columbia Journalism Review 196

V. Toward Greater Privacy

Editor's Introduction 200
Constance Holden. Fruitful Privacy Efforts of Congress
. . . . Science 201
Douglas W. Metz and George B. Trubow. The Com-
plexity of Privacy . . . . Trial 208
Henry M. Jackson. Privacy and Society . . . . Humanist 213
Gaylord Nelson. On Curbing Wiretapping . . . . Trial 220
Richard S. Jacobson. Citizens' Look at Privacy . . . . . .
. . . . Trial 226

Bibliography 233

I. PRIVACY IN A FREE SOCIETY

EDITOR'S INTRODUCTION

How great are the invasions of privacy in our society by government agencies and business systems employing computerized information techniques? Do Americans really value privacy? And do recent changing lifestyles in our society forewarn us that the concept of privacy as a cherished right may become outdated? These are some of the broader questions surveyed in this section.

The first selection is from the book *Dossier: The Secret Files They Keep on You,* by Aryeh Neier, executive director of the American Civil Liberties Union. Neier looks at a series of privacy issues today and recommends certain curbs on the compilation and use of government and business dossiers. The second article is a detailed inquiry into computerized information and the need for effective protection of individual rights. The authors are Marguerite Guzman Bouvard, professor of political science, and Jacques Bouvard, a computer scientist.

Two articles follow on the question, Do Americans value privacy? The first is by Arthur S. Miller, a law professor, and the second by Barbara L. Kaiser, an attorney and member of the Privacy Committee of the American Civil Liberties Union.

The last two articles deal with the impact of our evolving political/legal/cultural setting on the protection of privacy. Stephen Arons, an attorney and professor in a legal studies program, believes that we are seeing the rise of "police logic" that enlarges police prerogatives and diminishes the privacy of citizens in their cars, their homes, and their places of business. Thomas J. Cottle, of the Children's Defense Fund, points out that the ongoing social revolution threatens to make privacy impossible.

PRIVACY, SOCIETY, AND DOSSIERS [1]

The main protection for privacy in the United States
Constitution is the Fourth Amendment. It asserts "the right
of the people to be secure in their persons, houses, papers,
and effects, against unreasonable searches and seizures. . . ."
The authors of that guarantee remembered the "writs of assistance," general warrants authorizing wide searches. Armed
with such writs, British crown officers burst into the homes
and mercantile offices of the citizens of Massachusetts,
arrested the occupants, seized property in lieu of the payment of taxes and destroyed much of the remaining property. James Otis, assisted by the young John Adams, fed the
fires of revolution in Boston with eloquent arguments that
the Act of Parliament in 1699, purportedly authorizing the
writs, was "an act against natural equity" and, therefore,
"void. If an act of Parliament should be passed in the very
words of this petition for writs of assistance, it would be
void. . . ."

Today, the Fourth Amendment is most often invoked
to regulate contacts between the police and citizens on the
streets, in their cars and in their homes. It is the provision
of the Constitution most directly in controversy in debates
over "law and order." In 1961, a decision by the Supreme
Court, *Mapp v. Ohio,* made it applicable to the states.
Evidence seized illegally was no longer admissible in state
court criminal proceedings. For a very brief period, the
Mapp decision played havoc with the traditional methods of
local law enforcement officials accustomed to searching
people at will and prosecuting them on the basis of any
contraband or evidence discovered. However, with a small
exercise of ingenuity, police departments soon returned to
their old ways. State legislatures cooperated by enacting
"stop and frisk" laws, "no knock" laws, and other devices to

[1] From "Remedy," chapter 16 of *Dossier: The Secret Files They Keep on
You,* by Aryeh Neier, the executive director of the American Civil Liberties
Union. Stein and Day. '75. p 186-99. Copyright © 1974 by Aryeh Neier. Re-
printed with permission of Stein and Day/*Publishers.*

legalize random and instrusive searches. And, most important of all, police discovered that a little perjury would provide judges with what they needed to declare any evidence seized legally admissible. "As I approached the defendant, he became apprehensive and I saw him reach into his back pocket and drop something into the gutter," the officer testifies. This allows a prosecution for possession of drugs or gambling paraphernalia without any mention of a search. In the criminal courts, these are known as "dropsy" cases, after the peculiar malady of dropping things which began to afflict criminal defendants all across the country as soon as police recovered from the shock of *Mapp*. If evidence is seized from a person's home or car, the officer now testifies the search was based on "a tip from a confidential informant whose identity cannot be revealed but who has previously provided reliable information."

The Warren Supreme Court, author of the *Mapp* decision, started the process of eroding it by accepting some of these circumventions. The Burger Court has continued and greatly accelerated the process. As a result, there is no area of constitutional law today where the citizen can expect so little help from the courts as if he has a claim that his right to privacy under the Fourth Amendment has been breached.

Given the reluctance of the courts to enforce the Fourth Amendment in areas it plainly encompasses, there seems little likelihood it will be invoked to govern great intrusions in privacy never envisioned by its authors. In fits and starts, the courts have been willing to enjoin some forms of electronic eavesdropping under the banner of the Fourth Amendment and, even more rarely, some lower courts have invoked it against psychological questionnaires and lie detectors. But it is not a promising path for anyone interested in finding a way to curb most forms of dossier-building.

Other constitutional avenues are being explored, though not yet with any great success. The First Amendment's guarantees of freedom of expression and assembly are occasionally applied to the collection of data on political views and associations. The Fifth Amendment's guarantee of due process of law encompasses the presumption of innocence. A handful of court decisions have blocked the dissemination of arrest records not followed by convictions in an effort to make the presumption meaningful. And in a 1965 Supreme Court case, several justices found a protection for privacy in the Ninth Amendment: "The enumeration in this Constitution, of certain rights, shall not be construed to deny or disparage others retained by the people." The case, *Griswold v. Connecticut,* overturned a law against the use of contraceptive devices because it interfered with the privacy of the marital relationship. Citing the narrow protections for privacy derived from other amendments to the Constitution (including the Third Amendment's prohibition against compulsory quartering of soldiers in private homes in time of peace), the justices said that together, the Constitution forms a "penumbra" guaranteeing privacy. The Ninth Amendment guaranteed in broader terms rights such as privacy emanating "from the totality of the constitutional scheme under which we live," as Justice Brandeis stated it a generation earlier.

Despite the sweeping protection for privacy suggested by *Griswold,* its principles have rarely been followed. *Griswold* was the high water mark of the Warren Court's expansive reading of the Bill of Rights. In the intervening decade, the courts have backed away from the Ninth Amendment and its potential as a protection for privacy.

The word *privacy* never appears in the Constitution. It is only in the last century that this word has been used as a legal concept to describe the state's duty to let people alone. An 1890 article by Louis D. Brandeis and Samuel D. Warren on the right to privacy helped arouse interest. Many years later, as a justice of the Supreme Court, Brandeis championed privacy in one of the dissenting opinions for which he is principally remembered today. "The right to be let alone," said Brandeis in *Olmstead v. United States* in 1928, is "the most comprehensive of rights and the right most valued by civilized men." But he couldn't persuade a majority of his colleagues. Chief Justice Taft's opinion for the Court upheld the wiretapping of Olmstead, a bootlegger during Prohibition, because no "tangible" property had been seized and the eavesdropping was accomplished without a physical invasion of his property.

The Public's View of Privacy

Wiretapping and lie detectors provoked most legal debates about privacy prior to the 1960s. The few efforts to challenge dossier-building practices in the courts have been rebuffed. Judges resist the use of constitutional provisions to curb dossiers. Necessarily, advocates of controls must turn to Congress and the state legislatures. And that means public opinion must demand curbs.

Americans, most of whom have never suffered the indignities of police state invasions of their rights, have little fear of government dossiers—not just on criminals, but on them [said a Roper organization survey in early 1974]. The vast majority think it "appropriate" for the FBI to have on file about people like themselves such information as fingerprints, race, and birth date. They also think the FBI should have prison records, and arrests resulting in convictions . . . just over half of the public thinks the FBI should have psychiatric histories.

There are some limits on the information Americans think should be collected. Only 39 percent of Americans said the FBI should have records of arrests that do not result in convictions, and only 21 percent would allow the FBI to collect opinions of neighbors about individuals' moral character.

Americans are much less tolerant of data collection by private employers. Fifty percent would allow private employers access to conviction records, 38 percent to psychiatric records, and only 20 percent to records of arrest not resulting in convictions. By far the greatest resistance to data collection appears in response to questions about credit card companies. Only 15 percent of Americans would give them access to conviction records, 10 percent to psychiatric records, and a mere 8 percent would let credit card companies see records of arrests that don't lead to convictions. While the Roper survey does not exactly contradict George Bernard Shaw's insistence that Americans have no sense of privacy, neither is it cause for abject despair.

The public's willingness to allow the FBI to collect personal data reflects the bureau's success in portraying itself as a no-nonsense law enforcement investigative agency. Americans would be less tolerant if they knew that the FBI as a data collector serves employment agency and credit bureau purposes more effectively than it does the investigation of crime. And, it is good news indeed that most Americans have sufficient faith in the presumption of innocence to oppose giving records of arrests not resulting in convictions to anyone, including the FBI.

One disturbing finding by the Roper survey is the low regard for the confidentiality of psychiatric records. Still, only about half as many approve of collecting information about sexual history as psychiatric history: 24 percent approve of the FBI collecting sexual history, 51 percent psychiatric history; 5 percent approve of a credit card company collecting sexual history, 10 percent psychiatric history. These results suggest that references to psychiatric history conjure up images of psychopathic criminals or at least someone other than oneself—everyone has a sexual history. Occasional sensational publicity on crimes committed by ex-mental patients is highly misleading. Ironically, individuals who were patients in mental hospitals commit crimes much less often than other people do. If investigation of crime is the most widely accepted rationale for data-collection, logically, records on ex-psychiatric hospital patients should be compiled less readily than records on those never hospitalized.

Privacy is often, mistakenly, perceived as a predominantly middle-class concern. The Roper survey demonstrates that nonwhites accurately gauge how much of a stake they have in limiting dossiers. Nonwhites disapproved of the collecting of information about twice as often as whites.

Resistance to data collection is greatest when people feel that irrelevant data about their private lives influences their economic transactions. Blacks experience the use of irrelevant data against them much more often than whites.

Privacy and Job-Getting

The most important economic transaction most of us ever engage in is getting a job. We grow up believing, as the Bible tells, that, "In the sweat of thy brow shalt thou eat bread." What Richard Nixon called the "work ethic" and what we used to call the "Protestant ethic" dominates our society. Work, said Freud, gives a person a "place in a portion of reality." It also pays the bills.

Proposals for limiting the accumulation of dossiers should focus on protecting the right to work. That purpose would be served best if all dossiers . . . were assembled in one place and a fire set to the lot of them. Since such a drastic, simple, and effective approach is impractical at best, legal safeguards must substitute.

First, a warning: that word *safeguard* is dangerous. It implies that an instrument which can cause a great deal of evil can be so controlled that it causes only good. Usually, it doesn't work out that way. Man's capacity to devise safeguards is exceeded by his capacity to devise loopholes which defeat safeguards. A safeguard implies that its main effect is good. That is often quite untrue. Certainly, it is in this instance. The main effect of dossiers is baneful. Their purpose is to track what people have been doing with their lives, especially, what someone else thinks is bad. Even if dossiers are never used against a person, they restrict the sense of freedom. We know or suspect that institutions employ clerks whose job it is to prevent us from exceeding the limits set for us by our records. We lower our sights, in consequence, and conform to the dossiers.

When, at a 1973 meeting sponsored by the American Bar Association, I called for the destruction of dossiers, I was challenged by a Kansas prison warden. He argued for maintenance of records because the "records are earned." They are an important part of punishment for doing wrong, he said.

The Kansas prison warden made the most honest argument for keeping dossiers. Records kept and disseminated by such presumably benevolent institutions as schools and mental hospitals do not help the people they label, despite that avowed purpose. Nor do the records maintained by law enforcement agencies serve the investigative purposes claimed for them. They punish people, though the dossier compilers seldom admit this is the purpose or acknowledge that it is the consequence. Because they have such enormous punitive impact on their direct and indirect victims, I want to destroy the dossiers. . . .

Privacy for the Young

Most stigmas people acquire are pinned to them very early in life. This is one of the most important reasons for destroying records, it seems to me. School, predelinquency, and juvenile court records, and records of drug addiction afflict the young. Selective Service and military discharge records label the young. In 1971, 53.6 percent of all arrests were of persons under twenty-five. . . .

Dossiers are maintained in the belief that people who make trouble are irredeemable. That notion is contradicted by the natural and precipitous decline in troublemaking as people reach maturity. Elimination of the records would allow people to leave behind them the stormy years of youth. They would have the opportunity to enjoy the benefits our society has to offer. The end of records would help them adopt styles of life less threatening to the tranquillity of the rest of us.

But, since life is real and earnest, I suppose that the dream of a grand bonfire must be postponed.

A frequent proposal for curbing the use of criminal conviction records is to seal them, after a period of years. The biblically significant period of seven years turns up in bills introduced in Congress and in state legislatures. Examination of what happens to ex-convicts suggests that sealing records after seven years would benefit very few.

An FBI report on 18,567 offenders who had been released in 1963 showed that after three years 52.6 percent had been rearrested; after the fourth year, 60.9 percent; after five years it rose only slightly to 63.3 percent; and at the end of the sixth year it had only risen to 65.1 percent, an addition of just 1.8 percent. The study supports the common-sense proposition that an ex-convict needs the most help right after he has gotten out of prison If he hasn't been rearrested for six or seven years after getting out of prison, chances are he has rehabilitated himself or is so skillful a criminal that he doesn't get caught or that he is dead. Sealing the record of such a person makes little sense.

If a record is to be sealed or destroyed, it should be done immediately: right after acquittal, when a person gets out of prison or leaves a mental hospital.

The Need for Access to Records

The right to examine one's own record and challenge its accuracy is frequently proposed. If anecdotal records compiled by schools, mental hospitals, and credit bureaus were accessible to those whose names are on the file folders, the compilers would hesitate before including gossipy or false information, or unfair interpretations.

Access to one's own arrest records would allow the person not convicted to insure that the disposition accompanies his arrest record. An absolute prohibition on the maintenance and dissemination of arrest records that did not include disposition records would be more useful. Even better, would be a prohibition on keeping and distributing records of arrest of those never convicted.

The New York State Identification and Intelligence System [NYSIIS] permits people to examine their own arrest records. It works like this. A person goes to an office of NYSIIS in one of the state's major cities and submits his fingerprints. The prints are checked by computer against the six million in the NYSIIS data bank and, in a matter of moments, a printout informs the person of the record maintained on him.

Only a handful of people have taken advantage of the right to see the records maintained on them by NYSIIS, and no wonder. Not many people are willing to give a law enforcement agency their fingerprints in order to find out their records. It is the only way to get the facts, however, since this is how the NYSIIS files are organized. It is also the only way so far available to be sure the person sees his own record and not somebody else's.

The fingerprint data banks maintained by law enforcement agencies are, mostly, fairly accurate—incomplete and misleading because of their failure to note dispositions, but accurate. For a person with a record of arrest or conviction, the important thing is not to be judged by that record when seeking a job. Even the right to check or to complete the record may be insufficient because employers may be as reluctant to hire people acquitted of crimes as people who were convicted.

A giant step forward would be a prohibition on the maintenance of all arrest records not resulting in convictions. Most Western European countries do not maintain arrest records, though exceptions are made when a person already has a conviction record and then is arrested again but not convicted a second time. Says a recent book on British practices:

In the event of acquittal, the police generally destroy the data. . . . Some criminal record office spokesmen . . . insist that no form of "black mark" remains in their records as the result of acquittal. Other criminal record offices do retain certain information generated in prosecutions leading to acquittals . . . information may be retained after acquittal if the charges have involved matters considered by the police especially serious or especially

likely to be repeated, sexual offenses being the prime example.
(James B. Rule. *Private Lives and Public Surveillance*. New York:
Schocken Books. 1974.)

In the United States, it would simply not do to allow
this much discretion in record maintenance. Unless there
is express prohibition in law of the maintenance of arrest
records, they will be maintained. And, if there are to be
exceptions, a notion which flies in the face of the presumption of innocence, they too must be precisely described in
the law. A loose restriction such as "dangerousness" would
be interpreted out of existence. If legislators are to insist
on the maintenance of arrest records of persons charged
with child molestation or rape, those exact crimes should
be spelled out in law. It will be difficult enough to get law
enforcement agencies to comply with any laws restricting
record keeping; imprecision will greatly compound the
problem.

How to Prevent Data Dissemination

Laws which limit the dissemination of information, as
opposed to their collection, are attractive, but of questionable value. Once an information data bank exists, incentives
to get access to it appear. Sometimes restrictions on dissemination fail because administrators are corrupt. Examples
are the White House's use of Internal Revenue Service
data on its political opponents and the FBI's leaks to one
of the Bureau's principal congressional champions, John
Rooney, of embarrassing data on his political opponents.
Or, a legislature may simply drop the restrictions under
pressure of some economic interest. The bill adopted by
Congress to overturn Judge Gesell's decision restricting
FBI dissemination of arrest records to law enforcement agencies was sponsored by . . . [Senators Alan Bible and
Howard W. Cannon, Democrats] of Nevada. They were
representing the interest of their state's gaming industry in
access to the records. The New York law giving that state's
securities industry access to the state's criminal records sys-

tem to screen employees was lobbied through by the industry to counter bad publicity about losses of stocks. The securities firms sought to shift the blame for their losses, which resulted from sloppiness, to thieves they were first going to detect by fingerprinting their employees. The realities of bureaucratic practice also limit the value of restrictions on dissemination. The British criminal record offices, for example,

answer hundreds of telephone requests each day—the figure is in the thousands for the Metropolitan [London] office. . . . It is impossible to prevent in all cases the dissemination of such information to nonpolice callers, even though criminal record office staffs may do their best to do so. Virtually anyone familiar with the telephone number of the regional office and the routines for making such requests can eventually obtain the information he seeks: if not on the first try, then sooner or later. The vulnerability of these offices is especially great to former members of the police, who are invariably well versed in the techniques of making such requests. (Rule. *Private Lives and Public Surveillance*. Schocken. '74. p 82)

In the United States, also, industrial security jobs are dominated by ex-FBI agents and ex-policemen. Their training and their old friendships with colleagues still in law enforcement agencies get them the cooperation of those agencies.

It is impossible to police each agency privileged to receive data. Even if the FBI were to restrict the dissemination of arrest and conviction data to other law enforcement agencies, how could thousands of recipient police departments be checked to see they don't disseminate it further? The simple answer is that it is not possible. That is one reason the FBI has never even tried.

Notifying Dossier Subjects

An important reform would be a requirement that an agency which maintains a dossier notify the subject of the dossier every time it gives out information. The person could then counter discreditable information. If an arrest is reported, the person could explain the circumstances. If it is a bad credit rating, the person could explain that the merchandise was defective and, therefore, he refused to pay for it. If it is a school's account of radical political activities, the person could go to court to challenge the use of such data for employment purposes because it puts an improper price on the exercise of First Amendment rights.

Notification has been opposed because it is too "difficult" or "expensive." It is hard to take such arguments very seriously. As long as data are forwarded from one institution to another, it should be neither difficult nor expensive to send a copy to the person's last known address.

A less satisfactory procedure, though still a valuable reform, would require agencies disseminating personal data to publish guides to their procedures. A guide would contain a description of the data collected; the kinds of persons about whom they are collected; the sources of the data; the persons and agencies with access to the data; the circumstances of access; and the procedures that should be followed by someone who wants to see his own record and, if need be, correct it. A requirement that such guides be published would impose only minimal burdens on data collectors and, except for their desire to remain unaccountable, it is hard to imagine grounds for opposing it.

Another significant reform would limit the use of data. A law could prohibit the use of arrest records as a criterion for employment or continuing employment. On its face, such a law would be attractive. If there is a significant investigative purpose served by arrest records, which I very much doubt, that purpose could still be served. At the same time, at least in theory, the records would not deny people jobs.

The difficulty comes in practice. If arrest records are readily available, a law saying they cannot be considered in hiring would be hard to enforce. Most decisions about whom to hire are necessarily subjective. It would be difficult to demonstrate that an arrest record led to the denial

of a job. Only if it is used as a complement to a restriction
on the dissemination of data would there be any great
value in a law barring consideration of data.

The safeguards I have discussed have limitations when
considered alone; in combination they would have bene-
ficial impact.

President Ford on Privacy

There is a growing public awareness that something
ought to be done. It was expressed by President Ford in his
address to a joint session of Congress just three days after
he became President. "There will be no illegal tapings,
eaves dropping, buggings, or break-ins by my Administration," said Ford. "There will be hot pursuit of tough laws to
prevent illegal invasions of privacy in both government and
private activities."

Ford's statement raises the hope that the national revulsion against Watergate may provide the sense of urgency
needed to translate proposals for privacy laws into reality.
In a nation preoccupied with the pressing problem of
safety, many had believed that privacy was a luxury that
must be sacrificed to achieve that greater good.

Many . . . dossier-building practices . . . are motivated
by the desire for safety, yet they have helped to create the
very social dislocation and crime they are intended to combat. Millions of persons are labeled as pariahs by their records. The label is self-fulfilling. Unable to get jobs or
housing, harassed by officialdom, they have become pariahs.

It is urgent that we bring back into the social main-
stream the millions of these rootless and disaffected people.
We can recapture many for a constructive life. Our best
hope is to stop adding to the pariah population. We can
end the labeling of children as "disruptive" or "mentally
deficient." We can stop classifying people by their arrests
or "undesirable" discharges from the armed forces. We can
end the dossiers of misdeeds, real and alleged, that follow
us and our children everywhere.

COMPUTERS AND INDIVIDUAL RIGHTS [2]

When the Founding Fathers assembled to draft the Constitution of the United States, they did not anticipate the need to establish privacy as an inalienable right. However, because of the need to reinterpret democratic values in changing social contexts, the state of California amended its constitution in 1972 in order to list privacy as a fundamental right.

Privacy is not an abstract concept. It has meaning only in relation to a national culture, a particular political system and a specific period of time. It has become an issue in modern democratic societies which are characterized by large-scale, sophisticated bureaucratic structures and advanced technology in communications and information systems.

Technological development has been permitted to evolve without regard for its impact on our democratic political system. Twenty years ago, information about individuals was stored on paper in file cabinets. Information-sharing between federal agencies and/or private concerns was both expensive and time-consuming and hence limited. Today, thanks to advances in computer technology, public and private institutions collect, maintain and exchange vast quantities of personal information concerning the American people. Federal data banks in particular contain all sorts of personal data, sometimes of a most unexpected nature. The air force lists religious affiliations in one of its personnel files and the Department of Agriculture keeps a file on children of migrant workers.

Growth of behavioral research has encouraged data col-

[2] From "Computerized Information and Effective Protection of Individual Rights," by Marguerite Guzman Bouvard and Jacques Bouvard. *Society.* 12:62-7. S./O. '75. Published by permission of Transaction, Inc., from *Society*, volume 12, number 6. Copyright © 1975, by Transaction, Inc. Marguerite Bouvard is associate professor and chairperson of the political science department at Regis College in Weston, Mass. Jacques Bouvard is a manager in systems engineering with Honeywell Information Systems, Inc., in Billerica, Mass., and a lecturer in computer science at Worcester Polytechnic Institute.

lection and storage in a variety of institutional settings: government agencies, such as the Department of Health, Education, and Welfare (HEW), bureaus and centers within schools and universities, hospitals and private businesses. Continuing advances in computer technology make it increasingly possible to maintain extensive records of historical data on millions of people. Once captured and entered into a computerized data bank, this personal data can be retained forever. At a moment's notice, it can be retrieved and flashed across a city or around the world to a police cruiser, a credit officer or a prospective employer via worldwide networks of telecommunications.

Data Profile

The real impact of the computer goes far beyond these efficient archival and broadcasting capabilities. It lies in the computer's ability to transform a mass of raw data into meaningful and usable information. Advances in data management technology provide the means for organizing data banks so that each item of data can be cross-indexed with other relevant elements to form a context of interpretation. Random facts about an individual may appear meaningless or innocuous when considered in isolation. When aggregated and interrelated with other facts, they form a composite "data profile" from which one can draw conclusions and make decisions.

Unless this profile is reasonably complete and properly balanced, it may project a distorted picture of reality and lead to false conclusions and unfair decisions, which may have a devastating impact upon a person's life. The New York *Times* has reported the case of a person who became the object of mail surveillance by the Federal Bureau of Investigation (FBI) after she was found to have corresponded with the American Socialist party. In the context of the radical unrest of the sixties, this was sufficient ground for the government to suspect this person of subversive activities and treat her as a potential threat to the internal security of the United States. Different conclusions might have been drawn if it had been known that the suspect was a fourteen-year-old high school student researching the Socialist movement for a term paper.

Personal data within a file has a market value. It can be bought, sold, stolen or traded for other data. Police, license bureaus, credit reporting agencies, housing agencies, educational institutions and welfare agencies routinely exchange data with one another, although the concerned individuals are usually unaware of it. More than 60 percent of the federal data banks surveyed by Senator Sam Ervin's Committee on the Judiciary were found to engage in various data exchange programs. In many cases, exchanges between agencies, such as the Central Intelligence Agency (CIA), Internal Revenue Service (IRS) and the FBI, are performed without adequate audit trail procedures so that the original source of the data and the circumstances under which it was gathered cannot be traced.

Some data interchanges among agencies are clearly deceptive. The IRS and the Selective Service System share personal data with other agencies despite pledges of confidentiality on the forms used to collect the data. This is all the more serious in that individuals refusing to disclose this information are subject to criminal penalties.

Confidentiality

Standards of confidentiality vary among federal agencies and the information passed from one agency to another is likely to be handled in different ways. The Census Bureau is unique among federal agencies in maintaining strict confidentiality rules. While some agencies have been successful in establishing specific guidelines for maintaining confidentiality of information within their own operations, they have found it difficult to generalize these rules to their exchange of data with other agencies. The transfer of data between federal, state and local governments constitutes an even greater threat to the individual than the exchange of information between federal agencies. Local information handlers are more numerous and more apt to be insensitive to privacy concerns.

A major factor of the privacy problem is the absence of legislation and organizational rules ensuring privacy, confidentiality and due process to the subjects of computerized information. Data banks have been established at all levels of government, business and the military services without any real knowledge or concern for their potential impact over individual rights.

A survey of federal data banks conducted by the Senate Judiciary Committee listed 858 data banks operated by 54 executive branch agencies that contain over one billion pieces of personal data about Americans. Only 10 percent of these data banks have been specifically authorized by law, and more than 40 percent do not inform individuals that records are being kept on them. The existence of secret data banks, surreptitiously collecting data about innocent Americans, is not science fiction, but contemporary reality. Americans now face a double challenge: to develop a public awareness of the privacy problem and to establish appropriate procedures to regulate the use and dissemination of computer-stored information.

The spectacular advances in computer technology of the last twenty years have not ended. Within the next ten years, computer data processing price/performance is expected to improve by nearly tenfold over present levels. Industry experts also anticipate storage capacities to increase dramatically, by a factor of 100 or more, while storage costs will drop about 100 times below current figures. By 1985, on-line data banks, with capacities of ten to fifty trillion characters and retrieval time of a fraction of a second, will be in operation.

The privacy issue is all the more urgent because of the widespread use of information systems to administer services which many Americans consider essential to their well-being. Along with the values of a democratic system, Americans have constantly rising expectations in terms of medical services, health insurance, credit, family assistance and education. Those in search of jobs, credit, housing, welfare and other services must disclose extensive information of a private nature in order to obtain these benefits. This information further accumulates into the files maintained by various private and public institutions. Postponing attention to this problem may lead Americans to believe that an encroachment into their personal privacy is the price they have to pay to enjoy these services.

An even bigger challenge lies ahead with the proposed national health insurance program, which many people believe will be enacted within the next few years. Sensitive information involved in the patient-doctor relationship will be entered into computerized data banks. The prospect of this information becoming available, at the push of a button, to any terminal user connected with a data bank, unknown to the patient, is a frightening thought.

Most Americans support the concept of privacy with a sense that it is somehow related to other values, such as individual freedom or the pursuit of happiness. So important is the value of privacy that one can use it to distinguish between different types of political systems. In authoritarian systems, such as the Soviet Union, privacy is enjoyed by the Politburo, the highest organ of the Communist party and the source of all policy in that society. On the other hand, the Soviet citizenry is subjected to thorough surveillance. In liberal democratic societies, individuals enjoy privacy in order to pursue their happiness and interest groups enjoy privacy in order to form public consensus, resolve conflicts and promote the expression of independent ideas. The partial autonomy of individual, family, religious and corporate groups in a liberal society prevents total politicizing of life.

Value Conflict

Every democratic society develops particular privacy balances between the need of governmental agencies for privacy and the need of the free press and interest groups for knowledge of government operations. At any time in an open society, there are conflicts between values, such as national security (which requires a certain amount of secrecy), freedom of the press, the right to know and the right to privacy. Compromises between these conflicts of interest vary according to time and place. However, fundamental values of individual and group autonomy cannot be compromised without transforming the entire political system.

Privacy is the guarantor of individual moral autonomy, a basic value in a democratic system of government. Privacy can be defined as the right to control one's information system and one's physical being. The latter right has been traditionally conceived in American society as the right to be secured against unauthorized entries and seizures. Both rights are closely related to the principle of respect for persons. Both must be reinterpreted in the light of changing technological and social contexts. Typical of this kind of reinterpretation is the study conducted by the Hastings Institute concerning nonvoluntary use of psychoactive drugs and behavior modification programs for incarcerated people. To what extent do these programs constitute an intrusion into the personal privacy of inmates? Should inmates be given the right to refuse participation in these programs?

Privacy is violated whenever a person's moral autonomy or self-image are impinged upon, even without affecting his conduct. Altering an individual's self-perception against his will offends human dignity. If we are able to regulate a person's conduct or keep it under surveillance (as in the system of dispensing welfare), we are, in fact, curtailing his responsibility as a moral agent making free choices. This limits the options open to persons regarding their relationship with others, their physical mobility and their own self-perception.

Privacy, the control of one's own person and of the extension of one's person in the form of information, is at the basis of man's claim for human dignity. Information about a person is an extension of selfhood, for him to communicate or withhold as he sees fit. Even when an individual divulges personal information to receive certain benefits, such as credit or insurance or to win a lawsuit, he has a continuing interest in retaining control over that information beyond the original disclosure, and especially the right to decide whether this information should be communicated to third parties.

The notion of self is associated with a person's recorded history of his individual and social activities. Information pertaining to these activities should be distinguished by degree of sensitivity and treated accordingly. A student's course selection or grade records are administrative in nature, while his request for contraceptives or psychological counseling from a university health service should be considered sensitive and should be disclosed only to those with a legitimate need to know.

Recognizing this distinction is extremely important and must keep pace with the growing trend toward integrating information systems. Unless such precautions are taken, a student's records, including such sensitive information, may be routinely passed on to prospective employers and become part of his employee record. It is in such cases that the combination of information from various files will present an inroad into personal privacy. To lose control over one's record of activities or traits is to lose control over one's self. On the other hand, the notion of consent is made possible by the control of one's information. If the facts about a person are freely disclosed with the knowledge and consent that they may be shared with others, there has been no violation of privacy.

A person's control over personal information and access to and dissemination of that information are at the heart of individual autonomy. The relationship of individual autonomy to the functioning of an open society requires renewed attention and emphasis at all levels of civic education. Too often, because the values of privacy are not clearly

defined and are not sufficiently stressed, the young adult
concludes that institutional efficiency and society's "right to
know" are more important than his right to make decisions.

Individuals vs. Institutions

The privacy issue involves other concerns often emotionally associated with, but not actually included in the concept of privacy. People may feel threatened by the very existence of massive and efficient information systems even
though their privacy has not actually been invaded. They
are often concerned about the endless search for personal
data by social scientists, market researchers, opinion poll-
sters and the institutions that use this data. When the institutions seeking information also control funds, the threat
appears much greater.

A recent incident involving HEW illustrates this concern. HEW requested the New York City Board of Education to disclose personal information on its students for the
purpose of developing a new data bank. The data bank was
to identify the racial and ethnic background of pupils, their
language background and their ability to speak English.
When the school board insisted that it would supply such
information only anonymously or statistically in order to
preserve the privacy of the pupils, HEW threatened to withhold millions in federal funds.

Although people may charge institutions that operate
information systems with invasion of privacy, their real complaint is often about institutional power and its linkage to
possession of information. An issue frequently associated
with privacy is the relationship of the individual to any
large institution operating a data bank. A student who recently completed an independent study on privacy and
banking complained that while banking institutions are
able to acquire a great deal of information about their customers, the reverse is not true.

Another element in the privacy issue is the right to be
presumed innocent until proven guilty. An article in the

New York *Times Magazine* by Aryeh Neier, executive director of the American Civil Liberties Union (ACLU), documents the inability of a would-be cab driver to find a job
because of an arrest record. The record contained no information regarding disposition of the case, which was later
dismissed. It followed that person whenever he moved and
prevented him from finding employment.

While arrest records are frequently incomplete and inaccurate, the individuals concerned have no access to them
and no way to correct them or to know that potential employers have access to them. There are no criminal or civil
sanctions against misuse of records and no clear set of standards in any state as to which jobs should require review of
criminal arrest records. In cases of incomplete or inaccurate
records, the burden of proof often rests with the injured
party, rather than with the managers of a data system, who
should shoulder the burden.

Trust is at the foundation of cooperative attitudes toward government agencies and institutions in the American
political system. If people feel that the information they
divulge to the census, for driver's registration or for immi-
gration and naturalization will not be treated confidentially
or will be sold on the marketplace as a trivial commodity,
they may become alienated from the goals and operations of
institutions which are supposed to serve them and which
rely upon their support.

These concerns focus on the place of the individual in a
technological society and reveal, not that too much power
is held by too few, but that so little is held by so many. In
the relationship between individuals and organizations, the
scales are balanced in favor of the latter. A Canadian task
force on Privacy and Computers stated that the information
process is one way in which institutions learn more about
individuals, but individuals learn no more about institutions or even what institutions learn about them.

Concern for privacy is caught up in the more general
debate regarding the effect of technology on society. Some

contemporary thinkers share a pessimistic view of this relationship and conclude that what is technically feasible is
allowed to occur without regard for the consequences. Hannah Arendt, Herbert Marcuse and Lewis Mumford share
this attitude. At the other end of the spectrum are those who
argue with Alvin Toffler that technology has allowed the
individual a greater range of choice than he has ever enjoyed before, one that may even be bewilderingly broad.
They argue further that problems resulting from modern
technology can be solved by the use of more technology.
The privacy issue, however, will suffer from being em-
broiled in this debate. Since technology is here to stay, the
privacy discussion should not focus on its desirability, but
rather on finding ways to protect humanistic values and
goals.

Guidelines for Protection

Regulation of the use of digitally stored information is
in its early stages. However, general guidelines for protecting privacy can be articulated for handling personal data at
various stages of gathering and dissemination.

Data-gathering practices are related to the problem of
privacy insofar as they involve acquiring personal information from individuals, their neighbors or associates. The information gathered may be derogatory, inaccurate or clearly
irrelevant to the purposes of the data bank. In the absence
of guidelines, the individual concerned has no right of re-
dress. The law of defamation does not prevent derogatory
information from being collected or disseminated, provided
the information is true. Harmful information can be so
labeled only in the context of particular uses. Information
regarding a person's drinking habits or marital status, while
not harmful in itself, may prevent that person from acquiring a job when passed on to a prospective employer.

Most data banks operate without guidelines regarding
types of information to be collected in order to fulfill the
objectives of the data bank, and without provisions for in-

suring either the currency, completeness or accuracy of the information. In the absence of clear definitions of relevant information, there is little to prevent private organizations or government agencies from gathering more information than necessary. Some critics have charged the Census Bureau with securing information of more interest to marketing and manufacturing concerns than to the bureau itself; others have charged credit bureaus with maintaining incomplete information.

In addition to establishing standards of relevance, there is a real need to clearly define areas which may not be the subject of inquiry and to enforce these limitations. Any kind of information which could serve as a source of prejudice against individuals, such as race, religion or marital status, should not be gathered. The incident in which the New York City Board of Education resisted HEW's request for sensitive information about pupils is a clear case in point. Given the ease and speed with which information passes from one organization to another, it could become the basis for unjust discrimination.

There should also be an enforceable code of conduct for those who collect information. Often, investigators are sent out in the field without guidelines on how to conduct themselves or on how to insure confidentiality of the data they gather. Nor are there any rules regarding permissible sources of information. Investigators all too frequently rely upon hearsay and gossip in order to supply their needs. Recent legislation in the Canadian provinces of Quebec, Manitoba and Saskatchewan has provided guidelines for credit reporting agencies regarding permissible contents of personal reports, disclosure of information to subjects and methods of collecting information.

Once a data file is established, its contents should be subject to periodic review for insuring currency, completeness and accuracy of information. Legislation ensuring persons access to files containing information about them is sorely lacking. The Fair Credit Reporting Act of 1972 allows an individual to discuss the contents of his file when denied credit, but he may not personally review the file or clarify certain details by inserting his own account in the record. In the field of public education, there have been many cases in which parents were forbidden access to the educational records of their children by school officials and also cases in which a child's school records were given out to persons and groups outside the school without the knowledge or consent of the child or his parents. Legislation enacted in August 1974 is intended to correct this situation.

Currently, there are no provisions for expunging obsolete or correcting incomplete information on criminal records. In the absence of regulations regarding the use, completeness and accuracy of records, the individual must rely upon expensive and lengthy litigation to obtain relief. While free access of individuals to records maintained on them is an important step in the verification process, the burden of responsibility for accuracy and completeness should rest entirely with the user of information systems.

Before the right of access to files containing personal information can be secured, individuals must gain the right to be informed of the existence of any file containing information about them. Even when people are aware that information is being held in a particular institution, the transfer and sharing of data among agencies is usually accomplished on a discretionary basis and out of public view. Individuals who divulge personal information in order to obtain a benefit or fulfill a requirement may not discover that this information has been used by third parties in a wholly different context.

At the federal level, data dissemination is partially encouraged by pressures from the House Ways and Means Committee and the Senate Finance Committee calling on federal agencies, such as HEW, to make more productive use of their data. The massive FEDNET system, which was proposed by the General Services Administration in order to provide efficient and economical computer services, is a case in point. Privacy should not be sacrificed for the sake of government efficiency any more than other basic freedoms. Alan Westin [professor of political science at Columbia University and editor of *Civil Liberties Review*] suggests developing the right of waiver and consent through legislation, the requirement that personal information be passed along only when the individual concerned consents to the transfer.

These considerations point to the pressing need for a flow of information from the user to the subject of data banks. The individual American needs to be informed of the existence of data banks which contain personal information on him and of the extent of data dissemination. Above all, he needs the opportunity to exercise his informed consent. Equally important is the need for the managers of data systems to accept and enforce guidelines regarding data-gathering practices as well as data maintenance, dissemination and usage. The data gathered by the user should be strictly relevant to a clearly articulated purpose and checked for accuracy. The sources of information should be reliable and made known to the data subject.

Guidelines for data maintenance should include appropriate procedures to insure accuracy, completeness and currency of files. These should provide for periodic purging of obsolete information and the opportunity of the file subject to review and correct his record. In the absence of statutory regulation of data dissemination, the "need to know" of government agencies, credit bureaus and employers should be carefully examined and balanced with the right of the individual to monitor the flow of his personal records.

Legislation for Privacy

Perhaps because of Watergate, the 93rd Congress has been called the Privacy Congress. Although the Senate Subcommittee on Constitutional Rights, under the Committee on the Judiciary, and the House Special Subcommittee on the Invasion of Privacy have been investigating the problem of information systems and privacy for almost a decade, it was not until 1974 that legislation was passed which embodies some general guidelines for protecting privacy.

The executive has also become concerned with the privacy implications of its massive automated files. In 1973, a report entitled *Records, Computers and the Rights of Citizens* was published by the Advisory Committee on Personal Data Systems established by Elliott Richardson when he was secretary of HEW. The report suggests the enactment of a Code of Fair Information Practices for all automated personal data systems. Among the principles included in the code were the right of Americans to know about records held on them and to be involved in insuring the accuracy and currency of these records.

In February 1974, a Domestic Council Committee on the Right of Privacy was created by the President. The mission of the council is to study some of the more pressing privacy problems associated with automated files and to request ways of handling them. Among its action items for 1975 are a review of the growing use of the Social Security number as a universal single identifier and of policy regarding dissemination and use of federal mailing lists.

While these general guidelines for privacy rights may seem praiseworthy, any legislation which seeks to make them operative will have to be passed in a context of opposing interests. The August 1974 law governing access to educational records is a case in point. The Family Educational Rights and Privacy section of the Elementary and Secondary School Act prohibits federal funds to any educational institution that has the policy of denying or which effectively prevents parents of students from inspecting and reviewing any and all official records, files and data directly related to their children. It also restricts release of file documents to third parties without the consent of parent or student. [For further details on this legislation, see "Student Privacy Rights," in Section IV, below.]

The months of hearings which preceded enactment of

this law gave evidence of considerable controversy. Once the law was passed, many universities proceeded to remove letters of recommendation from files which would be open to their subjects. For these institutions, the principle of confidentiality of letters of recommendation is more important than the right of students to see their records.

Another bill passed in 1974 is intended to insure that some privacy protection principles be observed in federal data systems. According to this legislation, data files will be listed annually by type and general content in the *Federal Register* and also published in an annual data bank directory available to the public. Citizens will be allowed to examine and correct their records, and agencies must insure the accuracy and currency of the data each time it is used or disseminated. This legislation does not apply to law enforcement records and some military and civil service commission records.

Three significant privacy areas are still not covered by legislation: criminal justice records, data banks maintained by the private sector and state and local government responsibility for taxes and welfare records. Senators Sam Ervin and Roman Hruska introduced two criminal justice bills in 1974. They contained provisions for sealing an individual's record seven years after a felony has been committed and five years after the commission of a misdemeanor if there had been no conviction during those years, if no prosecution was pending and if the person was not a fugitive. The Hruska bill prohibited disclosure of arrest records to other agencies without a disposition of the case. Both bills were opposed by the Justice Department and the FBI and were eventually defeated. Presumably, incomplete arrest records will continue to hinder some Americans as they seek jobs, housing or credit. [For more detailed information see "The New Technology of Criminal Justice Administration," in Section II below.]

Despite this promising start in assuring citizen rights and despite a varied group of interests supporting vigorous legislation from the leaders of the computer industry and society of computer professionals, civil libertarians and constitutional conservatives, much remains to be done. A continuing national concern with privacy must be sustained if technology is not to outstrip our capacity to regulate it with timeliness.

DO AMERICANS VALUE PRIVACY? [3]

President Nixon's 1974 State of the Union message focused national attention on the need for more protection of personal privacy. One would think, with that imprimatur, that privacy is high on the hierarchy of values of the American people. For some, the answer surely is that it is. Even for most, if the question is posed in the abstract, the same answer would be forthcoming.

Privacy, however, should not be viewed in isolation from other preferences of people. When it conflicts with other values, chiefly economic well-being, then it likely will give way. If people have to make choices, probably most Americans would rather give up some or much privacy in order to gain what to them is the greater goal. Not that this is known through empirical data. For some reason (itself an interesting question), social and behavioral scientists have made few inquiries into the social or psychological bases for the desire for privacy.

For that matter, it is by no means a self-evident proposition that people, beset by the loneliness of living on a dying cinder in the midst of limitless space, prefer privacy over, say, the solace to be gained from the warmth of human associations. The tendency of Americans to form groups, noticed as far back as de Tocqueville, is testimony to a pervasive wish not to be alone.

    [3] From "Do Americans *Really* Value Privacy?" by Arthur S. Miller, a professor at George Washington University National Law Center. *Privacy Report.* No. 8:1+. Mr. '74. Issued by Project on Privacy and Data Collection/American Civil Liberties Union Foundation. 410 First St. S.E. Washington, D.C. 20003. Reprinted by permission.

Furthermore, as . . . [Dostoievsky's] Grand Inquisitor well knew, man cannot stand the intolerable burden of freedom. Few—only a few—would choose a Robinson Crusoe existence, either on a remote island or as hermits. Man is conformist, rather than individualist as the American myth would have it. The fear of freedom is greater than the desire for it. The Inquisitor said that man requires three things—miracle, mystery, and authority. It is these, rather than atomistic individualism, that drive man, particularly man in a mass society. Freedom, and that includes privacy, are of less consequence. Attainment of privacy means loneliness—precisely what most people likely avoid (if they can) as they would the plague.

A passage from B. F. Skinner's *Walden Two* is instructive; he has Frazier say:

> Most people live from day-to-day . . . They look forward to having children, to seeing their children grow up, and so on. The majority of people don't want to plan. They want to be free from the responsibility of planning. What they ask is merely some assurance that they will be decently provided for. The rest is day-to-day enjoyment of life. That's the explanation of your Father Divines: people just naturally flock to anyone they can trust for the necessities of life.

One need not wholly subscribe to Skinner's view to believe that he has placed his finger on a basic human attribute.

Legal, including judicial, interest in privacy coincides roughly in time with the closing of the American frontier. The seminal law-journal article on privacy, by Warren and Brandeis, was published in 1890, precisely the time that Frederick Jackson Turner said that the frontier had vanished. Since then the United States has become increasingly urbanized—and since then a right to privacy has been widely recognized in both the private law of torts and in constitutional law.

But, concomitantly with increasing legal recognition of privacy, there has developed a technological ability to invade it by a number of means heretofore not known. Data

on individuals is easily collected and as easily stored. The
National Crime Information Center in the Department of
Justice, for example, has become—or at least is well on the
way to becoming—a national data center in which information about millions of individuals, not all of whom have
ever been caught up in the administration of the criminal
law, is stored and disseminated throughout the country.
What this means is all too clear: What is technologically
possible will be done.

Privacy tends to get recognition and protection in the
law when the interests of the state are considered to be
furthered—or, at least, are not considered to be endangered.
That may be seen in a number of Supreme Court decisions.
Wyman v. James is an example. There the Court said that
a welfare recipient could not invoke the Fourth Amendment's provision against warrantless searches, when social
caseworkers wanted to scrutinize the way in which a recipient lived.

Some may think that the *Abortion Cases,* in which the
Court held that women had a constitutional right to the
privacy of their bodies and thus could get abortions on
demand, was a victory for privacy. Even there, however, the
Court's opinion by Justice Harry Blackmun is befogged
with improbable reasoning. Blackmun said that privacy was
a part of the personal liberty protected by the Fourteenth
Amendment (and privacy included the right of a woman to
control her body). Implicit in his opinion, however, is that
the private decisions of a woman (or women) can by some
means—by analogy to Adam Smith's "invisible hand" in
economics—be translated into the common good. This, as
Professor Harry Wellington of the Yale Law School has recently noted, is analogous to the substantive due process
decisions such as *Lochner v. New York.* In *Lochner,* the
Court at the turn of the century found a similar right of
freedom of contract in the due process clause and translated
that into the common good by preventing states from legislating on labor contracts.

In net, then, privacy in my judgment tends to be a value of the middle or upper classes in the United States, which is honored when it does not unduly intrude upon the prerogatives of the state. By no means is it an ultimate value. The desire for companionship, the fear of loneliness, far outweigh individual interests in privacy.

PRIVACY IS NOT SOLITUDE [4]

Professor Miller's article, "Do Americans *Really* Value Privacy?" (*The Privacy Report,* March 1974) suggests, without explicitly stating, that privacy is a spurious value in present-day American society. He asserts that people are essentially, in effect, not loners but herd animals; not individualists, but conformists. Privacy, he says, means loneliness, a condition intolerable to most people, and he quotes a passage from *Walden Two* in which a character describes most of the human race as content if they can live from day to day, unwilling to plan or take responsibility for their future.

It may or may not be an accident that B. F. Skinner's character comes out sounding like President Nixon, telling us that "most Americans are like children in the family." Certainly it is clear that Professor Miller has used the *reductio ad absurdum* to prove his case, and—as usual when this technique is employed—he has proved too much. The values of privacy that are the concern of civil libertarians do not deny, and are not inconsistent with the social values of companionship, mutual dependency within families, love, team sports, political activity and all the other things that people do, by their own choice, with other people. To value one's privacy enough to litigate over it, as in *Wyman v. James* or the *Abortion Cases,* one need not be an actual or potential

[4] From article by Barbara L. Kaiser, an attorney in Mamaroneck, N.Y., who serves on the Privacy Committee of the American Civil Liberties Union. *Privacy Report.* No. 10:7-8. My. '74. Issued by Project on Privacy and Data Collection/American Civil Liberties Union Foundation. 410 First St. S.E. Washington, D.C. 20003. Reprinted by permission.

hermit, nor even an admirer of hermits. (*Wyman* involved warrantless searches of welfare recipients' homes.)

The civil liberties concept of privacy embraces that area within the life of a person to which he can say to an intruder, "This is none of your business: Keep out." It becomes a true civil liberties issue where the intruder is the government, or where the government licenses the intruder in some way, against the will of the person intruded upon.

The limits to this area are necessarily fluid. In a real sense, we do not know where we want to put them until they are tested by the effort to invade. Professor Miller is right in believing that technological advances tend inexorably to narrow the defensible area. It is not only the Justice Department that has a compendium of data on private citizens. There is a Medical Information Bureau that dispenses data to insurance companies on the medical history of applicants for insurance. A television camera on a utility pole, using infra-red light, can look into darkened rooms and provide entertainment for policemen monitoring the picture without the knowledge of the room's inhabitants. It is discouragingly true that the invention has usually done substantial damage before the litigation can be started, let alone concluded.

But this is not to say that we are to let go of whatever it is that the Ninth Amendment and the Fourth, Fifth and Fourteenth Amendments can salvage for us against the contracting world and ever more inquisitive government. Professor Miller says that Mr. Justice Blackmun, in the *Abortion Cases,* implies that "the private decisions of a woman (to control her body) can by some means . . . be translated into the common good," by analogy to the vector effect of individual decisions on a "free" market in classical economics. His statement misses the point. It *is* the common good, without translation, that each of us should be able to make such decisions without being regarded as instrumental to some other end. Something may come of the sum of all such decisions—good or bad—but the privacy interest that *Griswold v. Connecticut* and the *Abortion Cases* tend to protect is precisely the right to act, in these areas, without regard to state interests as embodied in statutes, regulations, case law or other artificial utterances.

Finally, the need of people for privacy is not limited to the middle or upper classes, as shown by *Wyman v. James*. The need is perhaps most acute where the ability to achieve privacy is least, at the interface between the law-enforcement arms of society and persons accused of crime: mostly poor and nonwhite inhabitants of cities. The whole law of search and seizure expresses the never-ending efforts of members of these classes to safeguard to themselves a small personal enclave into which the minions of the law cannot peer. That people ask the courts to protect their right of privacy is as significant as that the right is hard to defend, and is a sufficient proof that there is a human need for privacy as fundamental and as real as the social needs that Professor Miller puts first.

THE RISE OF POLICE LOGIC [5]

The . . . years [1970-1975] have seen a decline of civil liberties in the American consciousness. During the same period the majority of the Supreme Court has shifted to the Right. Taken together, these two developments seriously weaken constitutional protections against the arbitrary exercise of police power. In the term that ended . . . July [1974], the Court—in three decisions largely unnoticed by the public—sharply restricted personal privacy and, in the process, expanded law-enforcement powers of search and seizure. It turned over to the police decisions that have traditionally been made by the courts and adopted what might be called police logic—a form of thinking which holds that

[5] From article by Stephen Arons, attorney, assistant professor in the Legal Studies Program at the University of Massachusetts at Amherst. *Saturday Review.* 2:12-13+. Ap. 5, '75. © 1975 by Saturday Review/World, Inc. Reprinted by permission.

crime detection is society's ultimate value and overriding priority.

The police did not invent police logic, nor are they the only ones who think in this way. It has crept into the patterns of thought of all of us, from the average citizen apprehensive about being mugged to the legislators who approve preventive detention or no-knock search laws. In fact, the retreat of libertarian thinking at the hands of police logic is so widespread that not long ago it was found in a series of opinion polls that if the Bill of Rights were up for adoption today, a majority of Americans would vote it down.

The rise of police logic means that the justifiable American anxiety regarding violent crime has been transformed into support for police practices contradicting the Constitution and holding only the remotest possibility for reducing crimes and the national insecurity. The recent Supreme Court search-and-seizure cases demonstrate how entrenched police logic has become. In the very sensitive job of steering a course between institutional police interests and the elimination of crime on one side, and the preservation of the privacy of ordinary citizens on the other, the Court has committed a fundamental error. It has turned the tiller over to the police.

Warrantless Searches

Decisions on the back-to-back cases of *U.S. v. Robinson* and *Gustafson v. Florida* were handed down on December 11, 1973. In each case the defendant was stopped while driving a car, arrested for driving without a license, and convicted of possession of drugs. The drugs had been turned up in warrantless searches of the defendants at the time of their arrests, before they were taken to the police station. James Gustafson, for example, was returning to his college dormitory with a friend when a city policeman stopped the car to "check it out" after he had observed the left wheels cross into another traffic lane. Asked for his license, Gustafson replied that he had left it in his dormitory room. The officer then arrested him and searched him thoroughly. The officer removed from Gustafson's pocket a cigarette package, which contained three marijuana cigarettes. Gustafson was found guilty of the possession of marijuana. A similar search in *Robinson*—in which the police officer testified, "I didn't think about what I was looking for; I just searched him"— disclosed fourteen capsules of heroin.

These are not the only times, of course, when the Supreme Court has approved a search without a warrant incident to an arrest. In previous cases, however, the Court had created an exception to the Fourth Amendment requirement of getting a search warrant only when an *emergency* situation was involved. In the 1969 case of *Chimel v. California,* for example, the Court declared that at the time of arrest, a policeman might make a warrantless search of the person and the general area in which he was found, either to seize evidence which might otherwise be destroyed by the defendant or to search for weapons in order to protect the arresting officer and prevent escape. The scope of the search was to be limited by what was *necessary* under the circumstances. In the *Robinson* and *Gustafson* decisions, such questions about the reasons for the search were not taken into account. The Court simply found, as a blanket rule, that whenever a policeman makes an arrest with the intent of taking the suspect into custody, the policeman may conduct a full search of the person arrested. Although those holding the majority opinion discussed the problem of the officer's safety in a custodial arrest, their decision does not make such inquiries relevant to the question of the legality of the search. In fact, Frank Carrington, executive director of AELE (Americans for Effective Law Enforcement, a law-and-order organization that submitted briefs in favor of the police position in these cases), described the decision as "sweeping" and the police safety argument in the opinion as a superfluous, "make-weight issue."

The Court's sanction of full search in custodial arrest surprised even Assistant Solicitor General Allan Tuttle, who argued the police case before the Court in *Robinson*. He was prepared to urge a narrow ruling that would have approved the search of Robinson as necessary and "reasonable" under the circumstances, but he found a majority that wanted to go beyond that to expand police prerogatives. Obviously, judicial activism did not disappear with the Warren Court, it just changed political ideology.

From some points of view, it cannot be denied that catching Robinson and Gustafson was good work done in a difficult world. After all, both defendants were in possession of illegal substances. By the same logic, however, it would also be reasonable police activity to conduct periodic house searches, to administer truth serums to suspects, and to tap the phones of all citizens, because such activities undoubtedly would uncover evidence of crimes or criminal planning. But these are not the rules by which the Constitution intended that police work be done. No matter how sympathetic to the difficulties of policemen's work one is, the logic of crime detection remains limitless in its ability to destroy privacy and civil liberties. In the oral argument before the Court in *Gustafson*, police logic crept in during the following exchange between Justice Thurgood Marshall and Deputy Attorney General Barry Richard of Florida:

Justice Marshall: "If a policeman says I spit on the sidewalk, he can walk up to me, arrest me, and search me?"

Mr. Richard: "If it were lawful to arrest for spitting . . . and if the officer does arrest the person . . . I would think it would be perfectly reasonable."

Justice Marshall: "Well, what protection do I have?"

Mr. Richard: "You need not spit on the sidewalk, for one thing, your Honor."

No matter that Justice Marshall retorted that he said he was *arrested* for spitting, not that he had actually spit on the sidewalk. The state attorney still appealed to the inquisitorial notion of purity: If you haven't done anything wrong, you have nothing to fear from a police search.

It is precisely against this sort of logic that the Fourth

Amendment's requirement of gaining a warrant for a search is directed. And even the exceptions to the warrant requirement established before *Robinson* and *Gustafson* insist that justification for the search must appear "reasonable" *before* the search, not after. Yet the Court has now abandoned the inquiry into reasonableness, claiming that all the reason needed can be found in the fact of the custodial arrest, even, in some states, for so trivial a matter as driving with a broken taillight.

The outcome of these rulings is the creation of a category of 93 million motorists—and additional millions of pedestrians—whose right of privacy will now depend on police discretion rather than on court discretion. Inevitably, those who will feel the greatest impact of this judicial recklessness are minority-group members and persons holding unpopular beliefs. In a study conducted at California State College in 1970, F. K. Heussenstamm sent a group of careful drivers out on the Los Angeles Freeway, each driving a carefully inspected car. Each car had a Day Glo orange-and-black Black Panther bumper sticker. The result was that drivers who had no previous citations received 33 traffic citations in 17 days for such things as "incorrect lane change," "driving too slowly," and "driving erratically." Heussenstamm concluded that it was "statistically unlikely that this number of previously 'safe' drivers could amass such a collection of tickets without assuming real bias by police against drivers with Black Panther bumper stickers."

Eliminating the Exclusionary Rule

At the heart of police logic, as exemplified by the *Robinson* and *Gustafson* decisions, is the desire to eliminate the exclusionary rule—a Fourth Amendment principle which states that courts shall not allow the use of evidence illegally procured. Had the court found that the searches in *Gustafson* and *Robinson* violated the right of privacy of the defendants, it is this principle which would have commanded that the evidence of drug possession be suppressed at trial. The long history of the exclusionary rule is based upon two beliefs: Excluding illegally seized evidence will act as the best available deterrent to illegal police conduct, and the integrity of the judicial system would be weakened by reliance on evidence seized in violation of the Constitution. The rule mystifies the public, because by releasing defendants it forces us to confront the fact that the civil liberties of ordinary citizens are most often upheld in situations where they seem to benefit "criminals." Obviously, it galls the prosecutor and the police because it thwarts the achievement of police goals.

Frank Carrington of AELE has called the exclusionary rule an "excrescence on the criminal justice system." The issue of abolishing it is at the center of a storm of controversy. Fourteen years ago, in *Mapp* v. *Ohio*, the Supreme Court concluded that years of judicial experience had proved the rule the most reliable way of deterring official lawlessness. Chief Justice Burger has now made clear that he is prepared to abolish the rule in favor of civil suits against the police; a healthy bite has already been taken out of it by the Nixon appointees in another major decision of this past Supreme Court term, *U.S.* v. *Calandra.*

On December 11, 1970, federal agents obtained a warrant to search the machine-and-tool company that John Calandra owned in Cleveland. The warrant followed the requirement of the Fourth Amendment in specifying the things to be seized: bookmaking records and betting paraphernalia. None was found. But in their three-hour search of Calandra's office and files, the agents found evidence relating to loansharking activities. The evidence became the basis of grand-jury questioning of Calandra, in which he refused to answer, claiming that the questions were based on illegally seized evidence which ought to have been suppressed. Both the federal District Court and the Court of Appeals found that the search was illegal in that the warrant itself was issued without legal justification and that the seizure of loansharking evidence would have exceeded the scope of the warrant even if it had been legally issued.

With the search clearly illegal from its inception the question for the courts was whether the exclusionary rule allows a grand-jury proceeding to use evidence seized in violation of a citizen's Fourth Amendment rights. The Supreme Court agreed with the two lower courts that the search was illegal but reversed the lower-court decisions. It refused to apply the exclusionary rule to grand-jury proceedings and decided, in essence, that the police may use the fruits of an illegal search as the basis of grand-jury questions and indictments. To put the implications of the decision in their plainest terms, the police may break into a citizen's home or place of business without a warrant or other legal justification, search the place completely, and use whatever they seize as a basis for calling the citizen before a grand jury and securing an indictment against him.

This evidence cannot, for the time being, be used in a criminal trial, and Mr. Justice Powell was quick to point out this fact in the majority opinion. But anyone who has been indicted or questioned by a grand jury knows that the consequences—even without a trial—are far from insignificant. In spite of these consequences, the Court allowed the use of the illegal evidence. What is striking and frightening about Powell's opinion is that it makes no mention of the possible loss of judicial integrity which results from a court's use of illegal evidence.

Perhaps this omission is part of a general governmental amnesia about integrity, to which Watergate attests. Or perhaps it is part of a conscious effort to purge from the legal doctrine the strongest roadblock to eliminating the exclusionary rule. In either case, a majority of those charged with interpreting the Constitution have managed to ignore a central principle of law and judicial integrity, stated most tersely by Mr. Justice Holmes in 1928: "If the existing code does not permit district attorneys to have a hand in such dirty business, it does not permit the judge to allow such iniquities to succeed."

Enlarging Police Prerogatives

Taken together, the *Robinson, Gustafson,* and *Calandra* cases substantially enlarge police prerogatives and diminish the privacy of citizens in their cars, their homes, and their places of business. Great claims have been made for the use of civil suits against the police for illegal searches, but such suits are extremely difficult to win; and leaving the citizenry with no other remedy than civil suits means, in Justice William Brennan's words, that "officialdom may profit from its lawlessness if it is willing to pay a price."

The short-term practical effects of these decisions unfortunately do not end the tale. Indeed, this tale may not have an end, for the dissenters in these cases—Justices Marshall, Brennan and Douglas—served notice in strong terms that a dangerous shift in ideology has taken place. It is rare to find a Supreme Court justice saying, as Mr. Justice Marshall says in his *Robinson* dissent, that the majority's "examination into prior practice . . . is not only wholly superficial but totally inaccurate and misleading." There is more here than mere doctrinal disagreement.

Nothing about these very difficult and delicate problems of reducing crime and ensuring privacy merits an attack upon policemen, their integrity, or their individual motives. More so than is true of our jobs, their jobs are caught between the contradictory demands of law and order. They work at a most difficult and generally thankless task. In order to survive in the police bureaucracy and in the public favor, the policeman must demonstrate that he can catch criminals, prevent crime, and be an authority figure in a society in which no one knows how to do these things. And he must wade daily through the seamiest situations on behalf of the public. In the words of Paul Chevigny, in his book *Police Power*: ". . . The police are a godsend, because all the acts of oppression that must be performed in this society to keep it running smoothly are pushed upon [them].

. . . The police have become the repository of all the illiberal impulses in this liberal society."

But there is definite cause for alarm when police logic becomes more persuasive in the lay and legal minds than are the principles of liberty embodied by the Bill of Rights. Forty-five years ago Ortega y Gasset wrote that it is foolish to imagine that the police are always going to be content to preserve order as defined by the government: "Inevitably they [the police] will end by themselves defining and deciding on the order they are going to impose—which naturally will be that which suits them best." It is this deference to police discretion that is becoming characteristic of the Supreme Court. It is up to the rest of us to bring this trend to a halt while it can still be done.

IS PRIVACY POSSIBLE? [6]

In the last decade, a decade some point to as a period of genuine social revolution, capitalism came under severe attack. At the most moderate and sanguine professional meetings, one heard references to changing the economic system, fighting the laws of private ownership. America needs changing from top to bottom, these people said. Money is the root of all evil and private ownership the ground in which this root grows.

But this is only part of the so-called social revolution, the part where the economically and politically minded enter. There is another part where the psychologically minded enter. And this part, too, has as one of its founding principles an abhorrence of what one might call the ownership of psychological property, or more simply, privacy.

It's peculiar, this psychological part of America's social revolution. It seemed to surface quietly enough, but grad-

[6] From "Exposing Ourselves in Public," by Thomas J. Cottle, author, associated with the Children's Defense Fund of the Washington Research Project. New Republic. 172:18-21. Mr. 8, '75. Reprinted by permission of The New Republic, © 1975, The New Republic, Inc.

ually, amidst a great deal of hubbub about the importance
of free expression, the release of the repressed, the necessity
to be open to everyone and to every experience, came a
new cry: let it all hang out! To have private thoughts, private emotions, was deemed as pathological as owning land,
a cotton factory and company store while others went hungry, unclothed, unsheltered. Now at these professional meetings where everybody agreed on the evils of capitalism,
they were speaking of the importance of spilling guts, bar-
ing souls, opening up fully to one another.

New businesses developed from all of this, and a new
professional cadre was born, seemingly overnight, to help
the rest of us uptight folks become downright loose. They
were telling us, this new cadre, that even if it meant taking
lessons or traveling long distances to special resorts and expensive retreats, it was essential that we learn to get those
inner feelings out of ourselves right there up front for
everyone to see, and hear, and touch. First the clothes, then
the easy feelings, then the tough feelings, the easy-to-tell
secrets, then the hard-to-tell secrets, then the entire inner
self. And when all this stuff had been exposed and we were
just about psychologically everted, the reality of psychological private property would be obliterated and we would
be free, or equal, or renewed, or something.

In the United States, the advice to the lovelorn columns,
and most conspicuously, the gossip magazine, gradually
turned the expression of private fears and wonderings into
a multimillion-dollar business. In the 1950s there was an exposé rage. Movie stars, the objects of our erotic and infan-
tile identifications, became the victims, along with athletes
and political figures. If persons did anything public, there
was no justifiable reason for them to claim the right to privacy at all. The exposé magazines got into bedrooms, Hef-
neresque industries undressed them, television and newspapers probed whatever was left. The more the probers
found, the better their audiences liked it, and strangely, the
more scabrous the reports, the more valid they seemed. An

article indicating someone to be a decent private citizen
was labeled a puff piece, the obvious product of a public
relations firm. Some of America's stars loved this sensuous
trespassing on their private property, some of them fought
against the exposure hounds, some were probably driven
crazy, to the point of suicide. What too many of the tres-
passers forgot was that even the most narcissistic of us occasionally needs to reflect on ourselves in private.

Then too, in the late 1940s and 1950s, there was the
paranoia about communism. So while some dug around
in the social lives of celebrities, others dug into files and
private papers and eventually into the ideologies, psycholo-
gies, philosophies, indeed into the very minds of men and
women. And what had been covered was undraped, what
had been silenced was made deafeningly loud, what had
been discreetly private was made outrageously public. At
that point an entire culture, just about, was involved in
erasing a significant boundary line between public and
private domains, between collective and individual existence.

Whether an individual has any right to privacy, or to
value privacy, was complicated not only by the press, but
by research findings. Countries have always spied on one
another, as have competing industries. Keeping watch on
next-door neighbors is no new business as Thorstein Veb-
len made clear, and as David Riesman in *The Lonely
Crowd* pointed out in his description of the other-directed
person. But in the last thirty years, an ethic of investigative
reporting has grown up in the enterprises of many researchers in the social and natural sciences. While some
scientists work, as we imagine scientists have always worked,
quietly, modestly, amidst their mysterious paraphernalia
and idiosyncrasies, others push for publicity, seemingly un-
affected by what personal hurt it may cause, or what ramifi-
cations their hunt for recognition has for them and their
talent.

Devaluation of Privacy

In the schools, there's been a revolutionary transformation in attitudes. Granted, public schools since the turn of the century have believed in personal development, discipline and getting along with others as major purposes of education. In the last decade, however, we have seen a colossal rise of a business known as psychology in the classroom, and the growth of an apparatus known as guidance counseling. In many affluent suburban grammar schools now, one finds compulsory sensitivity or human growth groups where children as young as six are obliged to reveal intimate feelings as well as their attitudes toward one another. In some of these programs, children earn points for their team merely by talking. Thus, tactiturn children run the risk of seeing themselves as troubled. And while children sit in their little chairs feeling the assault on their little psyches, their parents, in after-school programs—most of them, thankfully, voluntary—sit in their big chairs feeling the assault on their big psyches.

It all seems bizarre as one describes it, but the preoccupation with revealing and divulging has gone well beyond what many of us imagined. In California schools, professionals are beginning to diagnose a new childhood illness. It is called shyness, from the Middle English "schey," meaning timid. It has been deemed pathological, dangerous for the child. In some cases, drugs are administered to children to "open them up." In many schools, the value of individual study habits and working alone, encased in one's privacy, has been philosophically and architecturally precluded. Consider a simple question: what should children write on? A desk in which they can store their *own* belongings, or a table where space is shared with three or four other children? The presence of the desk or table bespeaks the value that a particular school places on individual learning or collective learning. While myriad factors affect the selection of desks or tables, open classrooms or closed ones, rooms without walls or spaces with built-in cubbies, one might discover that schools *without* desks are also schools *with* elaborate guidance personnel systems.

The increased use of mental health facilities in schools implies that certain educators believe that affective learning is as important in a child's development as cognitive learning. Once there seemed to be a distinct separation of the two approaches. One either advocated traditional pedagogic and traditional course work, or one argued for sensitivity training, psychological openness and the *feeling* of learning.

The disparity of philosophies partly reflected the traditional distinction between the family's role on the one hand, and the church and school on the other, in child rearing. It used to be the family's responsibility to shape the emotional life of children. Schools were for learning, the church for moral development. Now schools, with the influx of mental health workers and psychological researchers, are taking responsibility for cognitive, emotional and moral development. Families, too, have been pried open and their once private negotiations made public. Thus one finds school systems underwriting affective educational procedures, and in consequence, sensitivity training is valued in the same way as language arts, social studies and mathematics. One of the more distressing results of this human growth industry in schools and the more general popularization of psychology is that too many people have actually been trained to believe that only professionals can deal with their children.

The devaluation of privacy has meant other things for colleges. Many students complain of pressure to be intimate; there is no longer good reason, it is said, to postpone sexuality. One can put off work and ignore deadlines, but the time for complete openness and human sharing is now. The rules pertain to almost everyone. It is not enough to be an intellectual giant, or a simple teacher or learner. One's private life may be inspected at any moment and the search

for it called legitimate sociological inquiry. Those who
feel it is proper to divide their being into private and public sectors are called smug, traditionalist, uptight. The great
teachers, some would have us believe, make public all that
they possess, their knowledge and ideas, their families and
homes, their bodies and life histories. And evaluations of
other humans are eventually predicated on every sort of
in-class and out-of-class performance imaginable.

Psychotherapy and Privacy

In the practice of psychotherapy, a similar though frequently inadvertent attack on privacy has been lodged.
Medicine and allied fields of healing have always confronted
the question of which patients receive special treatment
and which ones can be used as case studies. Once it was
the rich, in their private rooms with private records and
as much anonymity as hospitals could muster, who were
allowed the greatest privacy. Public clinics meant public
knowledge of patient, illness, treatment. The poor were
used as specimen, display, experimentation. In mental
health treatment, this same pattern held. The names of
wealthier patients—those referred to as private patients—
were withheld from practically everyone; the names of clinic
patients were bandied about hospital meetings and social
gatherings.

Someone wrote that studying the poor is called sociol-
ogy, studying the rich exposé. This distinction may no longer
be valid, for now even the rich cannot be assured privacy
or immunity from being used as specimens. Similarly many
psychotherapists are revealing facts about their patients
even to the point that patients' identities can easily be in-
ferred. While confidentiality may be promised by psychotherapists, it is often not delivered. One hears stories of
video tapes of patients being played for audiences, some of
them not even professional therapists, without patients'
consent. One hears the spouse of a psychotherapist speaking
about patients, occasionally even by name. Indeed one

hears many patients speaking about their therapists. Apparently these people assume that their own psychotherapy is open for public consumption. Someone recently likened the announcement that one is entering psychoanalysis to the announcement of a child's birth: "With great pleasure and extreme humility, Thomas J. Cottle is proud to announce the birth of a 190-pound character disorder with underlying depressive reactions." Can anyone anymore assume confidentiality? Can anyone guarantee it?

Research subjects, too, are often left unprotected by investigators. Promised confidentiality, their names, interview protocols, test results are discussed in the cafeterias, offices and elevators of research institutions and universities. There are always the careful therapists and researchers who abide by the covenants of confidentiality and thereby honor privacy, but transgressors abound. Like adolescents experiencing sex for the first time, they must tell all.

If one recalls one's school days, the images of students daring one another to try something return rather quickly. Peer pressure isn't new. But it is now being intensified by the ethic to make the private public. Free speech has been turned on its head. Divulge and reveal are the battle cries. Nothing humans do must remain a secret; no one is to be reclusive, nothing about the body is to be mysterious. As the physiology and biochemistry of the brain are slowly, slowly understood, the contents of one's mind must be quickly, quickly reported. And if it takes drugs, electric shock, psychosurgery or some other form of artificial stimulation to open us up to new experiences, then we will embrace it, justify it. It's becoming so hard nowadays to keep a secret, to lose one's job or virginity, one's identity or sanity, one's health or loved ones, without writing a book about it. Holding things in is dirty, letting them out is cleansing. There can be no more fright, it is said, when one's inner world is seen in the light of day, in the presence of other people. When we tell everything no one can control us.

The Need to Reveal

One of the sad ironies of America's urge to expose everything and make privacy impossible is that people who think of themselves as anticapitalists have found a new commodity—the inner life—that is a marvelous source of profit. About the only book not yet written in that how-to-live-your-life category is how to survive the onslaught of how-to-live-your-life books. The sequel to Eric Berne's volume, *What to Say After You Say Hello*, might well be, *I'm Leaving Now; Hello Is All I Wanted to Say*. The new profit-takers of revelation may be fighting the old war horses of individualism and existential aloneness. Their hopes, presumably, are to replace these old spirits with a public effort at communalism, the sharing of all goods (and goodies) and services, and a society based on the collectivization of everything from family, to industry, to government to people's unconscious.

The danger lies in coercing people to reveal what they prefer to keep inside. The danger, as educators and physicians know, is keeping students' and patients' records private when the police, employers, armed forces and insurance companies insist on inspecting them. As an offshoot of the Buckley amendment ensuring students' privacy, we are seeing cases of corporations refusing to consider the job applications of students who do not allow prospective employers full access to their now "protected" college records. The danger is that with an enormous amount of information being collected by hundreds of agencies on millions of people, there will come a movement to predict behavior and to control it on the basis of what is predicted will happen. Without privacy and with open records, we will begin to treat people as *potential* psychopaths, criminals, delinquents, or assassins. This movement has already begun. We are less than a decade away from 1984. The danger is that the FBI and CIA will continue their spying on citizens, and that reputable newspapers, themselves decrying yellow

journalism, will print the findings that the CIA and FBI
uncovered but never made public.

The purpose of any sane political ideology should be
freedom for all human beings. In psychological terms, we
want all people to experience the feeling of freedom. In
many instances candor yields a wondrous sensation of being free. Unquestionably, people must be able to free themselves of ideas and emotions that trouble them and upset
their relationships with others, and which in many cases
confuse and damage institutions. Children should be allowed to safely reveal their problems to school personnel,
workers their inner worlds to one another and their bosses,
family members to each other. People do have a need to
confess or let others know bits and pieces of their private
lives.

The Need to Withhold

But if there is a need to reveal, there is also a need to
protect and withhold. Cards can be properly played close
to the chest. We make a mistake in forcing people to believe that every secret and sentiment, every inner inch of
ourselves, must be exposed. Freedom of speech shouldn't
be confused with perpetual human openness. One is not
attacking the concept of private ownership or safeguarding
the First Amendment by supporting publicness at all cost.
One is merely creating another artificial need; the need to
cleanse by candor and exposure. Watergate administrations,
foul dealing in industry, CIA interventions into foreign
countries, the oppression of peoples—these must be exposed and then expunged. But as the oppressed of the world
know well, freedom demands restraints. How many thousands of times one hears in conversations with the poor of
this land: "The government can make all the rules for living, but it will never tell me what to think, what to say,
and when to say it."

Sometimes the poor reveal an unmatched expressiveness and openness so dazzling that one feels they've never

known constraint. At other times, however, they strike that posture, that way of surviving-in-the-world called "cool." Suddenly the expressiveness and openness have vanished; we have no idea of what plays in their heads. We have no sense of their attitudes toward us, no idea of their plans. The cool ones, like the silent and reclusive ones, scare us. It is best to know where they stand, what they think, what they feel. When they reveal themselves, we have some hold on them.

A band of new profiteers is yanking us toward a world without personal protection, fences, shower curtains, clothes, a world of eternal lightness, without shadows, without night. Some of us prefer to hold onto a few secrets. We don't fear psychoanalysis stripping us of our meager bursts of creativity, we fear the ethic of publicness ripping away those private vessels in which the fluid of life is kept fresh, if not always pure. We fear a time when, after accommodating ourselves to nakedness on television, and then sex on television, and then sex in the midst of family therapy sessions on television, and then video tape feedbacks of ourselves watching sex acts among and between several species in the midst of interphylogenetic therapy sessions on television, the tube will suddenly glow white, and all the lights at home will glow bright, and the light outside will blaze, and we will see nothing and feel nothing.

II. GOVERNMENT AND PRIVACY

EDITOR'S INTRODUCTION

The federal government's general involvement with privacy issues is discussed in this section. (Section III is devoted to the Federal Bureau of Investigation and the Central Intelligence Agency.)

First, the new technology of criminal justice administration is considered by Mark H. Gitenstein, a counsel on the Senate Subcommittee on Constitutional Rights. FBI Director Clarence M. Kelley next looks at today's criminal justice information systems. Both articles address the impact of such technological systems on privacy matters.

The extent of electronic surveillance and wiretapping and the consequences for the individual's right to privacy are examined by Nicholas M. Horrock, correspondent of the New York *Times,* and by Robert Ellis Smith, editor of the *Privacy Journal.*

An article from *U.S. News & World Report* on the use of federal tax files concludes that "the blanket of secrecy in which Congress has wrapped tax returns since 1913 is in shreds."

Next, Morton H. Halperin, now associated with the American Civil Liberties Union and the Center for National Security Studies, contends that the Defense Department's National Security Agency (NSA) has become one of the most secret of the spy agencies.

Underlying much of the concern about privacy is the role police play in searches with or without warrants. The last article of this section, a two-part discussion, centers on this issue. An argument in favor of warrantless searches is made by Frank Carrington, an attorney and former law enforcement officer who is now executive director of Ameri-

cans for Effective Law Enforcement, Inc.; an opposing view
is given by Lloyd L. Weinreb, a Harvard law professor.

THE NEW TECHNOLOGY OF
CRIMINAL JUSTICE ADMINISTRATION [1]

On August 10th, 1965, a nineteen-year-old former ma-
rine named Dale Menard was arrested for burglary by the
Los Angeles police. Menard was taken to a precinct station,
booked and fingerprinted, but was subsequently released
because according to the police they were "unable to connect (Menard) with any felony or misdemeanor at this
time." For almost a decade Mr. Menard has attempted to
have all records of this unfortunate incident destroyed.

Despite the fact that the Los Angeles police admit that
Menard was involved in no criminal activity, it has taken
him nine frustrating years to get those records destroyed
and then only with the help of the federal courts. The problem is not only the reluctance of police to destroy even irrelevant records, but the fact that copies of the records have
been distributed outside the Los Angeles Police Department. Menard learned that his records were maintained not
only in Los Angeles and by state law enforcement officials
but also by the Federal Bureau of Investigation.

Furthermore, in the course of litigating the issues raised
by this incident and the aftermath of records, Menard and
his lawyers established that the criminal histories, so-called
rap sheets, maintained by local, state and federal police
were available to a variety of criminal justice and noncriminal justice agencies. They discovered that the Identification Division of the FBI, which maintained a copy of
Menard's record, operated without formal rules and routinely made its files available to organizations outside the
criminal justice community, ranging from the United States

[1] From "The Right to Privacy Is American," by Mark H. Gitenstein, a
counsel for the Senate Subcommittee on Constitutional Rights. *Trial.* 11:22+.
Ja./F. '75. Reprinted by permission of *Trial* magazine, © 1974, published bi-
monthly by The Association of Trial Lawyers of America.

Civil Service Commission to state and local organizations, such as bar admissions committees or taxicab license boards, and some private employers. Indeed, the federal judge who heard Menard's case, Judge Gerhard Gesell of the District of Columbia, described the record exchange system operated by the Identification Division as "out of effective control."

The Need for a National Policy

Menard's case is only the first of scores of complaints which have been brought to the attention of the Congress in . . . [recent] years. Judge Gesell in his critique of the system called on the Congress to adopt legislation which would create a "national policy" on the collection and exchange of "rap sheets" and other criminal justice information. These complaints and Judge Gesell's plea have been a major impetus behind the movement in Congress toward federal legislation which would formulate just such a national policy. However, these are not the developments which initiated congressional concern.

The fact that the Identification Division of the FBI maintains rap sheets on over 20 million individuals, 70 percent of which do not indicate any court disposition, and that half of the almost 30,000 daily requests to see these records are made by non-criminal-justice agencies for licensing or employment are themselves reason enough for congressional concern. However, this system has been operational for over fifty years without the precise sort of legislative guidance Judge Gesell has called for. It was the Justice Department's effort to automate these files beginning in 1969 which first prompted Congress's interest in this area.

It all began with a $4 million grant from the Justice Department's LEAA (Law Enforcement Assistance Administration) to a consortium of ten states which called itself Project SEARCH (System for the Electronic Analysis and Retrieval of Criminal Histories). The project did not use the FBI's files but the rap sheets of police in the ten co-

operating states. However, since the state files are identical
to those maintained by the FBI, that grant helped to demonstrate the feasibility of automating the FBI's files. Once
the Bureau saw that computerization was feasible, J. Edgar
Hoover proposed to Attorney General Mitchell that the
FBI operate the system as part of its National Crime Information Center (NCIC). Mitchell approved the FBI's request
over the strenuous objection of Project SEARCH, LEAA,
and the Office of Management and Budget, all of which
preferred a decentralized data system under the policy and
management control of the participating states to a national
databank operated by the FBI.

By 1974, LEAA had expended in excess of $300 million
on state and local criminal justice databanks based in part
on the SEARCH prototype and capable of instantaneous
data exchange with the new national databank operated by
the FBI's NCIC. A survey conducted two years ago by
LEAA found that there were over 450 automated criminal
justice databanks operated by state and local criminal justice agencies and funded in whole or in part with Justice
Department funds. The databanks contained information
ranging from "benign" files on criminal justice personnel
to extremely sensitive "organized crime intelligence." Indeed, in 1971 SEARCH began to develop a prototype for
the interstate computerized exchange of intelligence information called IOCI (the Interstate Organized Crime Index). At the same time the criminal history or computerized
rap sheets systems also were proliferating. The 1972 LEAA
survey found 104 computerized criminal history systems
operated by state and local police. By early 1974, computerized criminal history files at the FBI's national databank
in NCIC had grown to files on 450,000 persons with approximately 6,000 police agencies having access. The FBI
announced that its ultimate plan was to have criminal history files on over 8 million individuals in its computer by
1984, accessible to over 45,000 police departments around
the nation. The General Accounting Office estimated the

cost at well in excess of $100 million. Recent studies suggest that this estimate may be quite conservative.

The Congressional Reaction

By February of 1974 it was clear to many members of Congress that the technology was developing at an uncontrolled pace and that most state and federal legislators were not even aware of the issue. There was no explicit federal legislation authorizing the development of a national police databank, yet on the other hand there was nothing standing in the way of the development of such a system. While it seemed that this data exchange network could be immensely valuable to law enforcement, the dangers to the individual and society were not so obvious.

Congressman Don Edwards (Democrat, California) held exploratory hearings on the subject in 1972 and again in 1973 and made a number of legislative proposals only to see them severely criticized by the Department of Justice. It was clear that without the help and cooperation of the Department and the criminal justice community little progress would be made. Just as the Edwards Subcommittee was preparing for more intensive legislative activity in this area, its members were charged with the time-consuming responsibility of a presidential impeachment.

The first significant comprehensive Justice Department proposal was made in early 1974 when a task force of Justice Department officials, appointed by then Attorney General Richardson, released a draft bill which was subsequently introduced by Senators Hruska (Republican, Nebraska) and Ervin (Democrat, North Carolina), the ranking Republican and chairman, respectively, of the Senate's Constitutional Rights Subcommittee. At the same time Senator Ervin introduced his own bill, S. 2963, and announced hearings for early March 1974. These hearings and the subsequent Subcommittee analysis of these two bills represent the first intensive oversight by the Congress of the technological revolution in criminal justice information practices wrought by the Department of Justice. In the course of this study, members of the Subcommittee have begun to recognize the possible repercussions of computer technology in criminal justice administration, but their concern is not limited to the impact of computers. The Subcommittee has also studied the damage resulting from the dissemination of police records, whether automated or manual, upon the integrity and reputations of individual citizens, as well as the loss of autonomy suffered by state and local police when the police record-keeping function is centralized in the FBI.

Major Problem Areas for Legislation

The Subcommittee has isolated five major problem areas which legislation must address:

□ The *first* area concerns the inaccuracy and incompleteness of the records. Information available to the Subcommittee indicates that of the rap sheets on 20 million people in the FBI's Identification Division, approximately 70 percent are incomplete, in that arrests which are noted on the rap sheets do not show court disposition. A study conducted in California is even more disturbing. It suggests that even records with dispositions are not to be relied upon. Forty percent of the rap sheets in the statewide study which did have dispositions were inaccurate and in some courts in California, it found inaccuracies in 100 percent of the rap sheets sampled. The danger of having such records used for investigative purpose by police, plea bargaining by prosecutors, and sentencing by judges should be obvious. Yet a study conducted for the Subcommittee by the General Accounting Office suggests that thousands of such records are used for these purposes each day by federal, state, and local criminal justice personnel.

□ The *second* problem area is the manner of releasing this information outside the criminal justice community for employment screening, licensing, or granting or denying of governmental or private benefits such as credit. The use of inaccurate or incomplete records for employment screening could result in great injustice, especially if the prospective employee does not know the content of the record or, in some cases, even whether a record has been used against him. Above and beyond the importance of accurate and complete records, Senator Ervin believes law enforcement agencies have no business doing employment screening for private enterprise, especially via the use of records which were originally compiled for law enforcement purposes. The Subcommittee has statistics and studies demonstrating how rap sheets can undermine employment opportunities and the extension of credit. In most states there is no effective control over such use. Indeed, in many states there is no explicit prohibition of any kind on the noncriminal justice use of these records. In some states it probably is not even a crime for a police officer to sell rap sheets to the personnel officer at the local department store.

□ The *third* problem area is a bit more subtle. What are the risks inherent in the unbridled use of such records within the criminal justice community? As suggested above, there is the problem of using an incomplete or inaccurate record for subsequent arrests, plea bargaining, or sentencing. However, Senator Ervin is concerned that computerization of rap sheets might eventually mean that raw arrest records could be used routinely by police for the purpose of making subsequent arrests. In a recent speech on the Senate floor he remarked about experiments with computer terminals in patrol cars and hypothesized the situation where a suspect was being detained because of a raw arrest record for a crime for which he had ultimately been exonerated but whose disposition had not been correctly recorded in the computer. According to Ervin, "Obviously a suspect with his hands against the patrol car being patted down by an officer will not be able to convince that officer that an arrest record appearing on the patrol car minicomputer terminal is inaccurate or incomplete and that he was exonerated of the arrest and should not be arrested again."

Of course that assumes the officer even bothers to tell the
subject about the record appearing on the minicomputer
in the patrol car.

☐ A *fourth* area involves the use of intelligence and investigative files, and in particular the automating of such files.
Everyone deplores the release of such files from the criminal justice community. These past two years of Watergate
have made Congress painfully aware that raw intelligence
and investigative files in the hands of the wrong people, including some government officials, can result in grave injus-
tices to innocent people. As to the question of automating
intelligence or investigative files, Clarence Kelley, director
of the FBI, warned the Subcommittee as follows:

> I do not feel that any criminal justice agency should include
> criminal intelligence information in a system to which direct, un-
> checked access is given to other agencies, even though they be
> criminal justice agencies.
> Extremely sensitive criminal intelligence information is re-
> ceived from informants. Much of this information is so singular
> in nature that it would severely jeopardize the source's security
> if any participating agency could access the computer without
> demonstrating a need to know such information to the contribu-
> tor.

Director Kelley went on to describe hypothetical situations where unchecked access to an intelligence computer
by law enforcement agencies could jeopardize police cor-
ruption investigations or could be used against innocent
individuals.

☐ The *fifth* area is the most difficult, but probably the
most important, issue which Congress is facing with regard
to these record systems. All of the efforts to automate these
records and upgrade communications between criminal
justice, and in particular law enforcement, agencies contemplate a national clearinghouse or databank usually
within the federal government. To some members of the
Subcommittee on Constitutional Rights, centralization of
state and local law enforcement record-keeping functions
in the Justice Department raises grave states' rights ques-

tions. Most of the records presently maintained at the FBI are state and local records. What becomes of the privacy and security policies of each of the different states, when one person, be it the Director of the FBI or the Attorney General, can make unilateral decisions as to how these records are used within the federal government or by the state and local agencies tied into the national databank? Some criminal justice experts suggest that we will not need a national police force if all the nation's police interagency communications and record-keeping functions are centralized in the FBI.

Proposed Legislation

The Subcommittee staff has been using Senator Ervin's bill S. 2963 as the vehicle for its legislative activity and consultations with law enforcement agencies.

Apparently, the process of consultation and accommodation with representatives of criminal justice agencies is beginning to bear results. Project SEARCH, which has led the criminal justice community in development of both technology and privacy policy and is now composed of gubernatorial appointees from each of the fifty states, recently endorsed a staff redraft of S. 2963. SEARCH proposed eleven mostly technical changes which are presently being incorporated into the draft bill to be presented to Senators Ervin and Hruska for their approval.

The purpose of this bill is to provide a uniform body of law governing the exchange of criminal justice records, intelligence and investigative information, and the release of such information to the public. It sets out specific restrictions on the dissemination of such records or information to other agencies and creates a federal cause of action by an injured subject against an agency or employee of an agency violating these restrictions.

It addressed the five problem areas set out above as follows:

1. On the issue of accuracy and updating, it would create precise standards for the utilization of old or incomplete records. Incomplete records would be sealed or made inaccessible after the passage of a prescribed period of time. Each subject of a rap sheet would have a right to inspect and challenge the record and would be able to seek federal injunctive relief against any agency which failed to correct an inaccurate record.

2. The legislation would bar the noncriminal justice use of all but conviction records or records indicating that a charge was still pending. But even with these records the federal legislation would require explicit state legislative authorization before federally obtained records could be used for noncriminal justice purposes. This provision as well as the remainder of the act does not become effective until two years after enactment so that state legislatures will have time to act. As a general principle, the legislation would bar the noncriminal justice use of intelligence or investigative files except in the limited circumstances where an individual is attempting to obtain a top secret security clearance or is being considered for an appointment to a governmental position of high sensitivity. Even in these latter circumstances, the use of such information would only be permitted where the subject gives his informed consent. The latter provision is designed to discourage the release of investigative or intelligence information in circumstances similar to that of the Daniel Schorr incident, in which the FBI was ordered by a White House official to disclose information on Schorr to the President because the CBS [Columbia Broadcasting System] television newsman, a critic of the Administration, was allegedly being considered for a presidential appointment.

3. The SEARCH-approved draft also sets out standards for the use of criminal histories, investigative and intelligence files within law enforcement. For example, it restricts, though it does not prohibit, the interagency exchange of incomplete records for investigative purposes or for the purpose of making a subsequent arrest. It also requires that

intelligence or investigative files only be given to another law enforcement agency where the latter agency can point to "specific and articulate facts which taken together with rational inferences from those facts warrant the conclusion that the individual (about whom the information concerns) has committed or is about to commit a criminal act and that the information may be relevant to that act." This standard is borrowed from the Supreme Court's "Stop and Frisk" rule in *Terry v. Ohio* 392 U.S. 1 (1968).

4. The provisions on public release of intelligence and investigative files and limitations on their use within the criminal justice community have been described above. The legislation also would follow Director Kelley's advice on automating such files. Although it would permit an agency to automate its intelligence and investigative files, it would prohibit direct access to such computers by anyone outside the agency which automated the files. Although another law enforcement agency might be informed of the existence of an intelligence or investigative file it could not automatically gain access to the file.

5. The bill would resolve the management and policy development question by creating an elaborate administrative structure to interpret and enforce the provisions of the act and to develop policy for the operation of the national criminal justice information systems (NCIC and the Identification Division). These administrative provisions are designed to give state and local criminal justice agencies a formal role in the development of national policy in this area and to limit the federal role. The state and local role now is at best hortatory and always at the benevolence of the Attorney General or the Director of the FBI.

The administrative provisions create three levels of responsibility. First, each state participating in interstate exchange of records would be required to designate a new or existing agency within the state to be primarily responsible for implementing the provisions of the act within that state or of any similar state statute. Second, a federal board would be created composed of representatives of federal, state, and local criminal justice agencies and private citizens. State and local representatives would have a majority on the board since most of the records in question are the work product of state and local agencies. Third, prior to the promulgation of any formal regulations interpreting the act, the Board would be required to seek the advice of SEARCH, the National Conference of State Criminal Justice Administrators, the National Law Enforcement Telecommunications System, and other organizations composed of state and local criminal justice personnel who will have to live with this legislation if it is enacted. Furthermore, the legislation will limit the federal role by mandating that most of the state files maintained by the FBI be returned to the states of origin and that the federal government only maintain a computerized index which would point an inquirer to the state maintaining the record. It also provides that once this pointer system is established state laws on this subject shall take precedence over both the federal statute and other state statutes after records from one state are transferred to another state.

In conclusion, this legislation, if enacted, is not simply designed to protect the privacy and reputations of innocent individuals whose records are maintained by a national criminal justice databank, though that is one of its primary functions. The bill would also attempt to resolve the complex questions of states' rights and federalism raised by centralizing the record-keeping and communications function of state and local criminal justice agencies in the federal government. There is a tradeoff in the bill. It recognizes for the first time that criminal justice agencies need a system for the interstate exchange of information on criminal suspects and that the federal government may play a prominent role in that data exchange. But it also commands that if the federal government is to play such a role . . . traditional concepts of federalism and rights of the individual must be preserved. [The Ervin-Hruska bills were opposed by the Justice Department and the FBI and were defeated.—Ed.]

CRIMINAL JUSTICE INFORMATION SYSTEMS [2]

One of the most studied problems in American society today is that of the invasion of the right of privacy. Stories abound on the subject in the news media. Jurists debate the various legal questions associated with this complex issue. Both chambers of Congress have formed committees to explore constitutional rights, focusing on privacy. In addition, the President in early 1974 established the Domestic Council Committee on the Right of Privacy. Since each of us cherishes his privacy, the extensive study being afforded this issue is certainly merited.

When considering the issue of the right of privacy, it is particularly important to be reminded that this is not a new idea. In fact, this right lies at the roots of our American heritage. Incensed reaction to the continuous infringement on the personal liberty of our early colonists gave birth to this nation—and it has been the protection of our hard-won rights that has sustained our republic through nearly two centuries.

Freedom, of course, is what America is all about. However, to guarantee tranquillity for all, freedom must be regulated. Total freedom would be chaotic. Therefore, for the good of all, rules must be established and laws must be enforced. It is in this area of maintaining the peace that problems have arisen regarding the methods of enforcing the law and concerning the retention of criminal records. At the core of the problems lies the issue of the right of privacy.

Interestingly enough, this right is not defined nor specified in our Constitution. Yet, the principle of privacy per-

[2] From "But So Is the Right to Law and Order," by Clarence M. Kelley, director of the Federal Bureau of Investigation. *Trial.* 11:23 +. Ja./F. '75. Reprinted by permission of *Trial* magazine, © 1974, published bi-monthly by The Association of Trial Lawyers of America.

meates this document. Though privacy is not specifically mentioned, it is certainly a factor in the First Amendment (religion, speech, press, assembly); Third Amendment (quartering troops); Fourth Amendment (unreasonable search and seizure); Fifth Amendment (self-incrimination); and Ninth Amendment (rights enumerated in the Constitution not to be construed to deny or disparage others retained by the people). Therefore, to paraphrase my earlier statement, privacy is what freedom is all about.

In its more than sixty years of operation, the Federal Bureau of Investigation (FBI) has been acutely attuned to protecting individual rights and liberties. The right of privacy is—and has been—of importance to the FBI in all of its activities. For instance, FBI records contain a vast amount of information which, if improperly maintained and disseminated, could be the cause for genuine concern by those most interested in the right of privacy. Fully realizing this, the FBI remains keenly aware of the necessity to safeguard the data entrusted to our organization. In addition to protecting the privacy of persons by imposing strict controls over accumulated data, the FBI also confronts the issue in certain phases of its investigative efforts. The right of privacy is one of the factors concerning how penetrating an FBI investigation can be and to whom the results can subsequently be reported.

Information Systems

Criminal justice information systems are the target of those most concerned about the possibility of the invasion of privacy. Criticism is leveled at the types of information stored in the systems, the validity of the data, the necessity for the information, the dissemination of the material, and the eventual purging or retention of the information. While it is true that the majority of the records of the criminal justice profession are maintained in manual systems, it is also a well-known fact that computerized systems are being increasingly implemented at all levels of the profession. It is this spreading computerization, with its ability to provide rapid access to large amounts of information, that has produced most of the concern for individual privacy.

I believe that a look at the file structure of the FBI can provide an understanding of how the privacy issue affects the FBI and the rest of the criminal justice profession. The FBI maintains three basic categories of records: FBI Identification Records, investigative files, and the National Crime Information Center (NCIC).

When a person is arrested by local, state, or federal law enforcement agencies, fingerprints and arrest data are forwarded to the FBI, which uses this information to compile the person's Identification Record. Such arrest records (sometimes referred to as rap sheets) may later be used in identifying suspects, in locating fugitives, and in providing guidance in bail, sentencing, and probation matters.

While Identification Records do provide a valuable service to law enforcement, one problem exists: to be complete, the record must reflect the eventual disposition of the charges against the persons arrested. While arrest information is usually immediately provided to the FBI, the data concerning final disposition is much more slowly furnished—if at all. To minimize inequities that can arise when Identification Records are used for non-law-enforcement purposes, the FBI adopted a policy as of July 1, 1974, regarding the processing of these civil-type fingerprints. We have discontinued furnishing the inquiring agency any information regarding arrests that are more than one year old *unless* the disposition of that arrest is also shown on the individual's Identification Record.

Citizens should also feel encouraged to learn that since 1973 any person can request a copy of his own Identification Record. If he then questions the accuracy or the completeness of any entry on that arrest record, he can arrange for it to be amended by the law enforcement agency which furnished the original data.

The investigative files of the FBI contain the results of

our investigations into matters within our jurisdiction. These files are composed almost entirely of interviews of citizens, officials, and informants. Legislation is presently being proposed which would allow individuals to personally review FBI investigative files concerning them, to determine the accuracy of the information and request correction of any errors. While those advocating such legislation have the highest ideals, it would be virtually impossible for the FBI to function satisfactorily if subjects of investigative files are permitted to inspect their files. Persons, including informants, would no longer willingly provide information for fear their identity would be learned. In some instances, due to the serious nature of the case, the lives of individuals would be at stake.

National Crime Information Center

The third basic category of files maintained by the FBI is the NCIC, which is a computerized index of stolen property, wanted persons, and criminal histories. The system is an excellent example of how modern technology has been effectively and responsibly employed by law enforcement. Although only operational since 1967, NCIC has become one of the most potent weapons against lawlessness.

NCIC was developed with a full recognition of the necessity to properly regulate and control it. Today this computerized information system, operated under strict professional management and careful safeguards, serves the cause of better law enforcement with distinction and without abuse of privacy rights.

Despite its lengthy record of success, NCIC has received some criticism, the bulk of which has been aimed at the computerized criminal histories portion of the system. I believe the criticism is occasioned because the purpose of these histories is misunderstood. Their sole purpose is to speed up the criminal justice process by making needed information rapidly available.

In appearances before Congress and the public at large

during the past several months, I have endeavored to point out the vital function of criminal justice information systems in maintaining a free and just society. I have stressed insuring that appropriate controls are established to guarantee that the information in these record systems is not misused, that the right of privacy is protected.

Law Enforcement and Privacy Legislation

On March 7, I testified before the United States Senate's Judiciary Subcommittee on Constitutional Rights relative to a number of proposed privacy bills. The ultimate aims of the bills that I discussed were to protect the individual against improper use of information collected by criminal justice agencies, and I am wholly in accord with this basic intent. Together with all responsible members of the law enforcement profession, I welcome the creation of legal sanctions against misuse of criminal justice information. We are acutely aware that misuse of such data may be extremely injurious to an individual's reputation and welfare.

While I emphasized to Congress my support of the formalization and clarification of controls on criminal justice information systems, I also took the occasion to point out that certain aspects of the legislation under consideration did not appear to be in the best interests of law enforcement and society as a whole. I felt then, as I do now, that our zeal to protect individual privacy must be tempered with a concern for an effective system of criminal justice.

In respect to key issues raised by these privacy bills, I have opposed provisions calling for the purging of conviction records. There are, I believe, substantial reasons for preserving this information. For example, under these provisions, fingerprint records would be unavailable for future comparison purposes, and records of prior criminal activity would be unavailable for sentencing purposes.

It is my belief, too, that a criminal justice information system should be controlled and operated by a criminal justice agency and should not share equipment, facilities, or procedures with any noncriminal justice system in order to insure the security of the information and to protect the privacy of individuals about whom the information applies.

Furthermore, I am opposed to inclusion of criminal intelligence information in systems to which direct, unchecked access is given to other agencies, even other criminal justice agencies, unless appropriate safeguards have been provided. The unverified nature of much intelligence information, as well as its sensitivity, particularly from the standpoint of protecting the source, calls for restricted handling.

I have also questioned the wisdom of flatly denying criminal offender information to noncriminal justice agencies where there exist legitimate needs for this data, such as in determining access to classified and sensitive information or in determining suitability for federal employment.

Another key issue involves the sealing of records. Proponents of such a restriction would have criminal offender record information, such as fingerprint cards and rap sheets, sealed after a stipulated period of time and thus unavailable for use by even criminal justice agencies. The stated purpose of sealing is to prevent an individual's record from adversely affecting him in later years, possibly after rehabilitation. It is, however, my view that sealing against criminal justice agencies is unwarranted and would act as a serious investigative handicap. I am convinced that the investigative value of such records, when confined within criminal justice agencies, far outweighs the relatively small possibility of their misuse.

I also expressed to the Subcommittee my deep concern over proposals to impose on criminal justice agencies blanket prohibitions against using such modern technological advances as the computer. This sort of arbitrary restriction on progress makes little sense to me. Control—not denial—is the proper approach to the utilization of modern technology.

The Needs of Society vs. the Needs of the Individual

Before closing this discussion, we would do well to take an overall view of the situation. We must look at the best interests of *both* society and the individual.

The right of privacy does not mean that shackles must be thrown around the legitimate operations of the law enforcement officer. It also does not mean that a citizen can freely declare that his activities are free from scrutiny. No person in our society is above the law.

Historically, in America freedom has meant a balance of individual and societal rights. Never is it a question of one or the other, but both. The moment we lose this balance, our free society will be jeopardized.

Any criminal justice information system must give *equal* concern to protecting the rights of all individuals and to the necessity for law enforcement agencies to have all pertinent information to meet their responsibilities. This represents quite a delicate balance, but a balance that has to be maintained.

Just as each of us treasures his personal privacy, it is our obligation to respect the privacy of others. Likewise, because of our professional responsibilities, it is essential that we have access to all information that will aid us in providing criminal justice. The challenge of combating crime while giving utmost concern to personal privacy is certainly complex, but it is a challenge that must be successfully handled for the good of all.

THE SCOPE OF ELECTRONIC SURVEILLANCE [3]

From the advent of Watergate . . . , national attention has been drawn again and again to the question of electronic surveillance; the issue of exactly how much wiretapping and

[3] From "Electronic Surveillance: Scope of Wiretapping and Bugging an Issue of Rising Concern," by Nicholas M. Horrock, staff reporter. New York *Times.* p 16. F. 20, '75. © 1975 by The New York Times Company. Reprinted by permission.

bugging really goes on in the United States. Recent disclosures that the Central Intelligence Agency engaged in domestic operations and that the Bell Telephone System monitored calls have served only to increase interest in the issue. Indeed, the problem has caused enough concern in Washington that a federal commission has been appointed to investigate wiretapping [the Commission on the Organization of Government for the Conduct of Foreign Policy] and it is the subject directly or indirectly of studies by four congressional committees.

Today [February 19, 1975], Senators Edward M. Kennedy (Democrat, Massachusetts) and Gaylord Nelson (Democrat, Wisconsin) introduced a bill to limit government use of only one facet of electronic surveillance, the "national security" wiretaps and buggings. The bill would require court orders in this type of electronic surveillance.

Nobody knows how widespread unauthorized government electronic surveillance is. Virtually every federal investigating agency—the FBI, the CIA, the Drug Enforcement Administration, the Defense Intelligence Agency, the Secret Service, the Internal Revenue Service, the Bureau of Alcohol, Tobacco and Firearms, to mention only the large ones—has the capability for wiretapping or bugging.

With the help of federal funds from the Law Enforcement Assistance Administration, every police department of any significant size probably has some equipment or training for electronic snooping.

Under present law, the American Telephone and Telegraph Company and the other companies of the Bell System have complete freedom to intrude on telephone conversations to check the quality of service and the performance of employees and to stop fraudulent use of telephones. . . . [Early in February 1975] a telephone company aide told a House subcommittee that in fighting toll fraud alone the company listened to 1.5 million to 1.8 million calls between 1965 and 1970.

Legislation Seeks Curb

Congress began to get concerned about bugging and wiretapping in the mid-1960s and the first framework of legislation to control its use was included in the Omnibus Crime Control Act of 1968.

The 1968 law, in turn, has been molded by amendments and by a Supreme Court ruling to the following legal shape: In order for any federal or state police agency to use a bug or a wiretap in a domestic criminal or domestic intelligence case it must obtain a court order. That simply means the agency must convince a judge that there is probable cause to believe a crime is being committed and the police would be best aided in solving it by electronic intrusion.

Department of Justice officials report that in most federal cases this is not an offhand matter, and some judges demand to know such precise details as where the bug would be placed and the chances that innocent persons might be overheard.

In the case of court-ordered wiretaps or buggings requested by a federal agency, the agency must get the approval of the attorney general before it goes to court.

Moreover, if the suspect under electronic surveillance is not prosecuted within ninety days and the tap or bug is thus unproductive, the government must inform the person that he or she was listened to.

National Security Area

Current law is far more vague, however, in the area of national security wiretaps and buggings. First, no court order is required. A federal agency has only to get the written authorization of the attorney general in order to install a device. There is no time limit on its use and there are no criteria for determining whether it is really needed and no requirement to inform the persons under surveillance.

Present law virtually prohibits wiretapping or bugging by private individuals and strictly controls the manufacture of devices for these purposes. Indeed, it makes private electronic snooping a crime, but there are enough loopholes and exceptions in the law to allow private electronic surveillance to exist still.

In 1973, the year for which the most recent figures have been computed, courts approved a total of 864 applications for electronic surveillance from federal, state and local police agencies. The government does not have to make public the number of national security wiretaps or bugs it installs.

In hearings [in spring 1974] before a Senate Judiciary subcommittee studying wiretapping, former Attorney General Elliot L. Richardson estimated that the number of national security electronic surveillances being conducted at any one time was about one hundred. He said that the total started in the course of a year might be 150.

Mr. Richardson also pointed out that the government conducted far more wiretaps than bugging, which brings up . . . [another matter—the] placing of an electronic listening device in a room or other premises, often requires what government agents call a "surreptitious entry," that is, a break-in or trespass to place the bug.

Wiretapping, on the other hand, can be accomplished at a distance from the target telephone.

What concerns many in Congress and in the courts is the degree to which unreported electronic surveillance is conducted by federal and local police agencies. When J. Edgar Hoover was director of the FBI, high-ranking former aides have confirmed, he ordered taps removed when he testified before Congress so he could attest to a low number.

Moreover, many sources in federal and local agencies say, there has been substantial "wildcatting"—that is the placing of surreptitious taps by the police or federal agents for which they fail to obtain court orders.

These taps and bugs produce raw intelligence, which the police use to make arrests, and not evidence. "It's like having your own, very best informer," one federal narcotics agent said.

Why Illegal Wiretapping?

Why do law enforcement officials engage in illegal wiretapping? Why do they jeopardize the prosecution of criminal cases and their own jobs? These questions go to the heart of the main issue of whether electronic surveillance is valuable at all.

Former Attorney General William B. Saxbe testified at Senate Judiciary subcommittee hearings . . . [in spring 1974] that a ban on national security taps would "put us at some disadvantage, but we would live with it."

But other law enforcement officials publicly and privately disagree. They argue that the threats to the United States, both foreign and domestic, are so sophisticated and make such great use of modern technology that police agencies without some ability to monitor telephones and to bug rooms are disarmed.

"In counterintelligence work," a former Army agent said, "you're trying to prevent a crime that hasn't happened. You need the wiretap to know where your adversary is going and what his plan is."

But electronic surveillance has had ominous side effects when used against American citizens. No matter how radical their politics, it is with this type of snooping that the government has intruded most often into political matters.

The wiretapping of the late Reverend Dr. Martin Luther King Jr. was an example. Even if eavesdropping on Dr. King could be justified because of his own political activities, which many critics question, the eavesdroppers also overheard numerous private conversations between Dr. King and every major political leader in this country. What they said to him and he to them may well have been valuable political intelligence for then President Johnson. Whether Mr. Johnson learned of the material or not has never been confirmed, but the potential for political misuse was clear.

No responsible government official now advocates a total ban on electronic surveillance. But many in the executive branch and Congress agree that there have to be far more rigid controls over electronic intrusion into the private lives of citizens. Concern is not only with wiretapping and bugging as it is now known, but also with conditions as they will be as 1984 approaches.

For instance, most major cities are now linked by computers that transmit their data, much of it private, from one city to another. There is no clear legislation against tapping computer talk. New developments in telephone technology make it possible to intrude on a large number of lines with little mechanical effort and less manpower, and these are not anticipated in current law.

Though the government now prosecutes illegal wiretapping in the private sector, many in Congress believe the laws should be clarified and prosecutions more aggressive. Another proposal that appears to have growing support would require court approval for all legal government electronic surveillances, whether involving criminal cases or national security.

THE WIRED NATION: WIRETAPS [4]

A minimum of 1,052 wiretaps, which intercepted an estimated 1.9 million conversations, were installed throughout the country during 1974. *Privacy Journal* compiled the figures from . . . [June 1975] disclosures about the extent of electronic surveillance, prompted by congressional inquiries, two significant court cases and the national commission on wiretapping.

The American Telephone and Telegraph Company revealed to the commission at hearings June 27 that it has discovered 1,457 wiretaps on customers' telephones from 1967 to June 1974, including 1,009 illegal devices, about 83 per-

[4] From article by Robert Ellis Smith. *Privacy Journal.* No. 9:1+. Jl. '75 Copyright 1975 Robert Ellis Smith. Reprinted by permission. The author was formerly associate director of ACLU's Privacy Project, assistant director of the U.S. Department of Health, Education, and Welfare Office for Civil Rights, and at one time a *Newsday* reporter. He is now publisher of *Privacy Journal.*

cent of them in residences. AT&T said by far most of the taps involve marital discord; the Department of Justice estimates that about 75 percent of all illegal taps involve intra-family situations.

Still, AT&T reported, only 2 percent of the wiretap complaints it receives actually pan out.

The company told the commission that there were 84 discovered taps in the first half of 1974, making an estimated 168 taps for the full year.

Two days earlier, Senator Edward M. Kennedy (Democrat, Massachusetts) made his annual release of figures he is able to get from the Department of Justice on government wiretaps installed for national security purposes, which under the 1968 Omnibus Crime Control Act require the approval of the President, not a court order. The Justice figures showed 190 such national security taps in 1974, a noticeable jump from prior years when an annual average of 111 was reported.

The annual tally of court-ordered taps by the federal government and twenty-two states that authorize electronic surveillance showed 694 taps (574 by the states) in 1974, at an average cost of about $8,000 and an average length of twenty-six days. The survey is required under the 1968 act.

The total of 1,052 wiretaps, then, would not include unknown illegal taps; unreported government taps, especially those in jurisdictions without enabling statutes; "service monitoring" by telephone companies, wiretaps with the consent of one party to a conversation; nor suspected electronic surveillance of American citizens by foreign agents (see allegations in *Report on CIA Activities Within the United States,* June 1975).

Nor do the figures include microphone surveillance (bugging), which has been estimated to be as frequent as telephone interceptions. (There were forty-two such bugs installed in 1974 for national security purposes.) Research by Herman Schwartz, professor of law at the State University of New York, Buffalo, has estimated that an average of

70 conversations are overheard per day on a federal wiretap. Assuming an average of 26 days, as in the case of court-ordered taps, that would mean a total of 1.9 million conversations overheard in known taps in 1974. The FBI reported to the national wiretap commission, established under the 1968 act to study the law's effect seven years later, that it had been receiving each year about 520 complaints of illegal taps by nongovernment parties until June 1973. Since then, the yearly average has jumped to 763. The FBI didn't say so, but the marked change occurred since the time that televised hearings and press reports exposed Watergate abuses.

Two Recent Court Cases

While commission members, including Cornell Law Professor G. Robert Blakey, author of the 1968 provisions, criticized Justice for its infrequent prosecution of illegal tapping cases, two court cases were revealing how the Department conducts its own wiretapping.

A former FBI agent detailed how Bureau clerks sit at library-style tables all day, headphones over their ears, reference books by their sides, listening in on the FBI's highly secret warrantless national security taps in the old Post Office building two blocks from the White House. The disclosures came in depositions in the damage suit by Morton Halperin, former National Security Council staffer subjected to warrantless taps for twenty-one months from 1969 to 1971. (*Halperin v. Kissinger*, CA 1187-73 [D.D.C.]).

Halperin contends that the Nixon taps were illegal because they were not prompted by legitimate concerns for national security and thus, under the 1968 act, require approval of a court or the consent of one party.

The Nixon Administration sought to have the warrantless "national security" provision include government taps of dissident domestic groups until the Supreme Court rejected that theory in 1972. The United States Court of Appeals in the District of Columbia has further refined that provision by rejecting Nixon Administration contentions that the national security exemption would allow warrantless taps of a domestic group if the tap were related to foreign affairs and foreign intelligence gathering. The target was the militant Jewish Defense League. The court said a court warrant was necessary unless the target was a foreign agent or a group collaborating with another nation. (*Zweibon v. Mitchell,* 73-1847. June 23, 1975.)

Attorney General Edward H. Levi said present US wiretap policy complies with the court decision, but precision on the extent of government wiretapping is difficult to achieve. The House of Representatives impeachment study revealed last year that J. Edgar Hoover would regularly order several FBI taps disconnected just before he was scheduled to testify before Congress each year on the number of taps presently in place.

Wiretap Loopholes

After studying for eighteen months and hearing testimony from prosecutors, judges, the Department of Justice, the telephone company and equipment manufacturers, the National Commission for the Review of Federal and State Laws Relating to Wiretapping and Electronic Surveillance has focused on several weaknesses in the wiretapping authority established in 1968 (18 USC 2510):

☐ The law permits electronic surveillance with the consent of one party, and this, according to some commissioners, has allowed manufacturers and investigators to deal in surveillance equipment that they claim is intended for consensual tapping, but in fact is used for illegal nonconsensual taps.

☐ The kind of devices that are "primarily useful" for surreptitious interception and therefore prohibited (Sec. 2512) is hard to define.

☐ The act bans interception of "wire or oral communications," thus not deterring interception of data communications, an increasingly prevalent practice.

□ The "national security" exemption needs tightening, in the light of Nixon Administration practices.

□ The federal government itself, through the Law Enforcement Assistance Administration, funds an estimated 75 percent of police department purchases of surveillance hardware, including some purchases in jurisdictions without wiretap authority in their laws.

SNOOPING INTO TAX RETURNS [5]

Reprinted from *U.S. News & World Report.*

The long-held notion that an individual's tax return is a private document, held in strictest confidence by the Internal Revenue Service, is turning out to be a myth.

Each year, increasing thousands of returns are drawn from the IRS files for inspection in investigations that have nothing to do with tax enforcement.

Now, legislation is shaping up in Congress, pushed by the Administration, to restore some of the tax privacy intended by Congress when it enacted the personal income tax back in 1913.

Under present ground rules, a new study suggests, it is hard to imagine a situation in which a federal agency cannot get a tax return, and get it with a minimum of ceremony. . . .

[In 1974] despite efforts by Internal Revenue Commissioner Donald C. Alexander to resist the trend toward routine breaches of tax privacy, federal agencies demanded—and got—nearly 30,000 tax returns filed by more than 8,000 individuals. That excludes the thousands of returns used more impersonally by the Census Bureau for statistical studies.

[5] From report entitled "Who's Snooping Into Your Tax Returns Now?" *U.S. News & World Report.* 79:61-2. Ag. 11, '75.

Congressional committees, too, enjoy easy access to tax returns, with no formalized rules to make sure that staff members keep the data confidential.

The House Internal Security Committee has examined the tax returns of Students for a Democratic Society, the Black Panther Party, the New Mobilization Committee to End the War in Vietnam, the Progressive Labor Party and the returns of officers of these groups.

The Senate Committee on Government Operations has used tax returns for investigations of riots, civil and criminal disorders and campus disturbances.

The Nixon White House staff used tax returns against political "enemies."

State and local officials get tax returns on magnetic tapes on a regular basis that offers IRS no effective way to monitor the use of the information by thousands of officials.

These are some of the facts disclosed by a comprehensive study done for the Administrative Conference of the United States by Meade Emory of the University of California, a visiting professor of law at Georgetown University.

Mr. Emory has reported on his findings in testimony before the Ways and Means Committee of the House and in talks with *U.S. News & World Report.*

Some federal agencies, Professor Emory notes, enjoy blanket authority to invade the tax-return files. Others must submit specific requests signed by the head of an agency and, in theory, give a detailed explanation of the need. In practice, little explanation is given.

Almost any individual might discover that his tax return is being pored over by one official or another—if he could just peek into the proper federal office.

The Civil Service Commission uses tax-return data to investigate job seekers. The Veterans Administration uses returns to check the income of pension claimants.

The Federal Housing Administration looks into the eligibility of families for housing assistance by inspecting their income-tax returns.

Returns have been examined by the Federal Communications Commission in ferreting out "payola" taken by disc jockeys, and by the Federal Home Loan Bank Board to determine whether activities of savings and loan associations and their staffs violate federal laws.

The Securities and Exchange Commission is a regular user of tax returns in its surveillance of stockbrokers.

The Small Business Administration wants, and gets, tax data to decide on the merits of loan applicants—and to assist in pressing for loan repayments.

Safeguards Bypassed

The Privacy Act of 1974 provides that no federal agency "shall disclose any record . . . to another agency, except pursuant to a written request by, or with the prior written consent of, the individual to whom the record pertains."

But the law also provides exceptions that are being used for what Professor Emory calls the "freewheeling disclosure of tax returns."

The Fourth Amendment safeguard against invasion of privacy and the Fifth Amendment privilege against self-incrimination also have failed to keep tax returns in the hands of the Internal Revenue Service.

Outside of IRS, the biggest user of returns for routine law-enforcement purposes—as distinguished from investigative purposes—is the Social Security Administration.

Professor Emory points out, however, that much of that use is designed to aid the taxpayer—for example, to establish his pension claim when his employers have failed to pay his Social Security tax.

Easily the biggest users for investigative projects are the Justice Department and US attorneys, for whom doors to the tax-return files are wide open. Treasury regulations provide that a return "shall be open to inspection by a US attorney or by an attorney of the Department of Justice where necessary in the performance of his duties."

Increasing resort to tax returns by [the Department of]

Justice, Professor Emory has shown, began in the early 1960s with the creation of interagency "strike forces" to investigate organized crime and racketeering. The hundreds of IRS agents serving on strike forces in eighteen cities provide tax-return data that is looked to for "leads."

Over the years since 1960, rivalry between the strike forces and US attorneys prompted ambitious prosecutors to set up their own "task forces," which have made increasing use of tax returns. . . . [In 1974] US attorneys inspected more than 18,000 individual returns.

In such investigations, reports Professor Emory, tax violations are only incidental factors in the drive for convictions in nontax crimes. Often, he says, the returns are inspected not for any investigation under way but for clues that might lead to an investigation. He told Congress:

"In many instances, the Department of Justice, for example, is using tax returns and tax-return information simply to conduct a fishing expedition, a use which cannot be regarded as consistent with the basic confidentiality to which returns are entitled."

The violation of privacy, Mr. Emory observes, is compounded by the free use made of the returns of individuals other than the persons under investigation.

Form 1040, filed by 80 million taxpayers each year, is an open window into the lives of individuals and families, says Professor Emory.

Aside from census information . . . tax returns probably constitute the single most complete source of information about our population in general and individuals in particular. As such, its existence has proven tantalizing to other governmental agencies.

Before the first seven questions have been answered, the taxpayer's name, address, Social Security number, marital status, and the number of children or other dependents and their names have been revealed. The next eight questions . . . lay bare the taxpayer's entire gross income, at least in summary form. Thus, before one has reached the first half of the first page of form 1040 much of the taxpayer's personal and financial life is exposed.

By checking other pages and schedules of a return, Professor Emory notes, an investigator can learn all about whether the individual or his family is under medical or psychiatric care, the organizations and causes he supports, the sources of his loans, his investments, union membership and many other details of his life.

Finally, a Change

While the erosion of tax-return confidentiality has been growing for years, it took the Watergate revelations about White House abuse of tax privacy to arouse Congress.

Now, the House Ways and Means Committee is planning to give a privacy-tightening measure priority over its tax-reform bill in the hope of getting final action by Congress—or at least by the House—by year-end [of 1975]. On July 8, Treasury Secretary William E. Simon told the Committee that secrecy-tightening proposals submitted by the Administration last September [1974] are being revised and will be resubmitted shortly. [As of February 1976, the measure was still in committee.—Ed.]

During the August recess of Congress, now begun, staffs of the tax-writing committees of Congress are to draw up legislation for the Ways and Means Committee to take up after Labor Day.

The measure is expected to require tax-return requests to be supported by more detailed statements justifying the inspection, to restrict blanket-authority privileges and requests for third-party returns, and to provide standards to limit the use of returns to the purposes for which they are released.

Backers of the legislative drive hope that, when tax-filing time comes around . . . [in 1976], people will be able to count on increased confidentiality for the information they are compelled by law to supply the IRS.

THE NATIONAL SECURITY AGENCY
AND DOMESTIC SPYING [6]

We now know that agencies presumed to be protecting the United States from foreign threats have in fact used some of their resources to violate Americans' constitutional rights. The army conducted an extensive surveillance of individuals opposed to the Vietnam war. The CIA, in operation CHAOS and other programs, spied on "dissident" groups. Domestic organizations such as the IRS and the FBI have also strayed from their responsibility to enforce the law, violating constitutional rights by snooping and, in the COINTELPRO [Counter-Intelligence Program] activities of the FBI, by seeking to manipulate the actions of groups. We have discovered all of this because of leaks from officials, investigative reporting, lawsuits filed under the Freedom of Information Act, and congressional investigations. [See Section IV, Individual Privacy Cases, for further information.]

There is, however, one organization whose intrusions into the private activities and communications of American citizens we are only beginning to glimpse. The National Security Agency (NSA), buried deep in the Defense Department, remains behind the curtain of official protection that in the past covered all intelligence organizations. Consider its position:

☐ Although it employs more people than the CIA does, its charter remains totally secret, as does its budget.

☐ NSA is completely exempt from the provisions of the Freedom of Information Act, which has been used to pry documents from the FBI and the CIA.

☐ Disclosure of the secrets of NSA is a criminal offense

[6] From "The Most Secret Agents," by Morton H. Halperin. *New Republic.* 173:12-13. Jl. 26, '75. Reprinted by permission of *The New Republic* © 1975, The New Republic, Inc. The author, a former senior fellow at Brookings Institution and consultant to the National Security Council, sued government officials for bugging his telephone. He is now associated with the American Civil Liberties Union and the Center for National Security Studies.

with no requirement that the government prove intent to injure the national defense as it must do for airing secrets of the CIA and Defense Department.

All of this seemed reasonable if the agency had limited itself to its primary function: the making and breaking of codes. Of all the institutions gaining respectability during World War II, the code breakers stand close to the top. It's well known that Japanese codes were cracked with a great impact on the battles of the Pacific. Only recently have we learned that the most secret codes of the Nazi high command were read throughout the war. No enemy has been shown to have broken any important American code.

This was an impressive record and Congress responded by tightening the laws making the release of codes or cryptographic information a crime. In the early 1950s, NSA was created in great secrecy by a still-classified presidential directive. Until recently the government would say nothing about what NSA does except for one enigmatic statement in the official government manual. Indeed it has been reported that one of the main government objections to the release of the Pentagon Papers, pressed in in-camera proceedings in the attempt to get an injunction against publication, was that it revealed the simple fact that the United States intercepts coded messages of foreign governments. The NSA budget is kept secret, hidden within the budget of the Department of Defense, of which it is nominally part.

As long as NSA remained out of the domestic affairs of the nation, there was little reason to object. Recently, however, there have been disturbing signs that NSA, like the other intelligence organizations, has over the years turned at least some of its attention to the political activities of American citizens.

The first tantalizing clue, virtually ignored at the time, came with the release of the so-called Huston Plan documents, relating to the White House proposal to step up surveillance of domestic "dissidents." Copies of these memoranda, taken by John Dean as part of his effort not to be a fall guy, revealed Nixon approval of a widespread program of illegal activities. Public attention focused on whether the plan actually went into effect not on the description of the current and past activities of the intelligence agencies. It was not known at the time that the memoranda were inaccurate, disguising existing violations of the law, a matter to which I return below.

Although the memorandum written by the interagency committee shows NSA to be an active participant in the discussions and its director, Vice Admiral Noel Gayler, as a signer of the report, we do not know what the report says about NSA activities since the entire discussion of its activities is deleted even from the most complete text available, that published by the House Judiciary Committee in its remarkable *Statement of Information Regarding White House Surveillance Activities* (Book VII). However the discussion of this subject in White House aide Tom Huston's memo to President Nixon, printed in the same volume, provides the first official clues to NSA activities. Here is what Huston wrote to the President regarding NSA:

Recommendation: Present interpretation should be broadened to permit and program for coverage by NSA of the communications of US citizens using international facilities.

Rationale: The FBI does not have the capacity to monitor international communications. NSA is currently doing so on a restricted basis, and the information it has provided has been most helpful. Much of this information is particularly useful to the White House and it would be to our disadvantage to allow the FBI to determine what NSA should do in this area without regard to our own requirements. No appreciable risk is involved in this course of action.

On July 23, 1970, Huston sent a memorandum to the heads of all intelligence agencies, including NSA, reporting the results of their exercise. The memorandum, whose subject was given as "Domestic Intelligence," listed a number of changes in procedures that the President had approved.

The first item reads as follows:

(1) *Interpretive Restraint on Communications Intelligence.*
National Security Council Intelligence Directive Number 6
(NSCID-6) is to be interpreted to permit NSA to program for
coverage the communications of US citizens using international
facilities.

Even in documents labeled "Top Secret Handle via
COMINT Channels only" (*i.e.*, via NSA channels) there is
ambiguity. Communications "using international facilities"
clearly refers to telephone, telegram and teletype messages
sent by American citizens to other Americans or foreigners
beyond the borders of the United States.

The implication of these documents is that while NSA
had the capability of monitoring the communications of
Americans, it was doing so, if at all, only to a very limited
degree. In fact that was as incorrect as the assertion in the
same documents that the CIA opening of overseas mail had
come to a halt. The intelligence community was apparently
not prepared to inform the White House, or at least Tom
Huston, of all that it was doing at the time. How much
others in the White House knew cannot be established from
these documents.

Information from the Rockefeller Commission

NSA in 1970 was engaged in its own massive illegal domestic surveillance operation on the international communications of American citizens of interest to the CIA
operation-CHAOS people. The description of that operation
in the Rockefeller commission report is worth quoting in
full because it is the only description we have of what NSA
does and is capable of doing in monitoring international
communications:

In addition, Operation CHAOS received materials from an
international communications activity of another agency of the
government. The Operation furnished a watch list of names to the
other agency and received a total of approximately 1,100 pages of
materials overall. The program to furnish the Operation with
these materials was not terminated until CHAOS went out of
existence. All such materials were returned to the originating

agency by the CIA in November 1974 because a review of the materials had apparently raised a question as to the legality of their being held by CIA. The materials concerned for the most part antiwar activities, travel to international peace conferences and movements of members of various dissident groups. The communications passed between the United States and foreign countries. None was purely domestic.

There can be no doubt, given Huston's memoranda, that the "other agency" is NSA. Given a person's name it can, apparently without monitoring that individual's home or office telephone, record and transcribe at least some of his or her international communications. That would mean that NSA does, as is often rumored, record all international communications leaving the United States (as it records all Soviet coded communications). Computer means must be available to scan those conversations and pick out those of interest to NSA.

Indirect confirmation of the existence of such a technical capability came with the release of the Colby Report sent to the President . . . [in December 1974]. Attached to the letter is a Colby memorandum of May 1973 ordering the agency to limit its activities in a number of areas. One of the attachments to the 1973 memorandum seems to confirm that the CIA has assisted in the development of computer technology for reading voices from tape. It authorized the CIA to continue to cooperate in such research but not to actually read any tapes itself.

What is of interest to the agency?

NSA is in large part a service bureau responding to the requests of others. For the CIA CHAOS operation, it spied on the communications of the antiwar movement. The information collected must have related in large part to legal political activities fully protected by the Bill of Rights.

If NSA performed this service for the CIA CHAOS program, surely it was available to other parts of the CIA, to the FBI, DIA [Defense Intelligence Agency] and to the armed service intelligence organizations. And what about the White House? Recall Huston's remark that "much of this information is particularly useful to the White House," and consider the interest White House political types had in various kinds of international communications—the telephone calls of members of Congress, the cables of journalists, the teletypes of businessmen. A shrewd NSA director could provide the White House, presumably on a White House—only basis, with a continuing stream of valuable political intelligence. Should one doubt that successive directors of NSA have understood this potential? Huston's comment suggests not.

All of this activity is a clear violation of the Fourth Amendment, which bans unreasonable searches and seizures and requires a court order before conversations can be intercepted. Americans are fully entitled to the protection of the amendment even if their conversations leave the bounds of this country. They are entitled to constitutional protection against actions of the American government even if they are themselves overseas.

President Ford has, according to the White House press spokesman, directed the attorney general to obey throughout the country the recent District of Columbia Circuit Court opinion that warrants are required for all wiretaps on American citizens who are not agents of foreign powers. The first question to ask is whether this directive applies as well to the activities of the National Security Agency. The Senate and House Intelligence committees should pick up where these clues leave off and see that NSA's spying on Americans is fully exposed. Then Congress must legislate to end abuses.

POLICE SEARCH WITHOUT WARRANT [7]

1. AN ARGUEMENT IN FAVOR [8]

On December 11, 1973, in the case of *United States v. Robinson* (and a comparison case *Gustafson v. Florida*) the United States Supreme Court upheld, by a 6 to 3 vote, the right of police officers to make a thorough search of persons lawfully arrested and taken into custody. If such a search reveals evidence of other crimes, the court held, this evidence may be used against the arrested person even though it has no relation to the crime for which the original arrest took place. These cases involved men lawfully arrested for traffic offenses who were taken into police custody and found to be in possession of narcotics.

The American Civil Liberties Union and similar groups, predictably, hit the ceiling, complaining that the ruling "infringes upon individual rights." The media, in many instances, fueled these cries by the manner in which they reported the decision. The *Robinson* decision, then, deserves some analysis in order to put it in its proper perspective.

First, the court limited its holdings to those cases in which the suspect has been *lawfully arrested*. If the arrest is not lawful—either because it was not based upon probable cause or because the arrest was used as a mere pretext to search—then no evidence turned up in a search incident to the arrest may be used against the accused.

Next, the court ruled only in cases of persons lawfully arrested and taken into custody. The court did not say that anyone who is merely stopped for a "routine traffic offense" and given a notice to appear in court may be thoroughly searched. To justify the extensive search permitted

---

[7] Article entitled "Courts Search Decision—Two Views." *Christian Science Monitor.* p F 8. Ja. 11, '74. Reprinted by permission from *The Christian Science Monitor* © 1974 The Christian Science Publishing Society. All rights reserved.
[8] By Frank Carrington, attorney, former law enforcement officer, now executive director of Americans for Effective Law Enforcement, Inc.

by the court, the offender must be taken into custody—
i.e., taken to a police facility for booking.

Critics of this decision have apparently come up with a
new "constitutional right" for those lawfully arrested: the
"right" to conceal contraband or evidence of all sorts of
other crimes upon their persons and to force the arresting
officer simply to close his eyes to such contraband or evidence. Following this novel theory, a person who had been
arrested for, say, nonsupport and taken into custody for
that offense, and who had in his pocket a gun which had
killed three people, would have a "right" to have the gun
suppressed—that is, the gun could not be used against him
in a prosecution for the murders.

But, say the critics of the search ruling, the decision will
lead to all sorts of abuses. This argument begs the question
completely. Any police power is subject to abuse, but this
does not mean for a moment that law enforcement officers
should have no powers at all. If and when a case of a
policeman's abusing his authority under the court's ruling
arises, then that officer should be dealt with swiftly and
firmly.

The search ruling is actually nothing new in our criminal justice system. One Supreme Court justice, in 1968,
acknowledged that a search incident to a lawful arrest can
". . . involve a relatively extensive exploration of the person." The justice, Earl Warren, certainly was no hard-line,
law-and-order conservative.

Finally, we are assured by the decision's critics, the ruling will be used by the police to harass minority citizens.
It should not be, and I believe that it will not be, so used
by the great majority of decent honest policemen in this
country. The poor and powerless of this country are "harassed" to a far greater extent by street criminals and dope
pushers than they are by the police. The *Robinson* rule
reaffirms for law enforcement officers a much needed, and
perfectly proper, legal tool with which to deal effectively
with those who prey upon the law-abiding, particularly the

minorities. It is an affirmation by the Court that the victims of crime in our society have some rights too.

2. An Opposing Viewpoint [9]

Strictly as a matter of constitutional doctrine, the Supreme Court's recent "traffic search" decisions do not break new ground.

The authority of the police to search a person whom they arrest is a settled exception to the Fourth Amendment's requirement that police officers search only pursuant to a warrant. Since the arrests of the defendants in the two cases, both for driving without a license, were valid, the searches that followed look as though they fall within the arrest exception to the general rule. In both cases the search turned up narcotics. The defendants were appealing from a conviction for a narcotics offense. But so long as the search was proper, the rule allowed whatever the police found to be used in evidence.

If one looks through the doctrinal smokescreen which the Supreme Court majority painstakingly sends up, the cases, *United States v. Robinson* and *Gustafson v. Florida,* have disquieting implications, and their consequences will serve none of us well whatever our attitudes to "law and order."

As recently as 1969, the Supreme Court explained why searches are allowed without a warrant following a lawful arrest. In order to make the arrest effective, the police officer must be allowed to search for weapons and means of escape; also, the court said, he must be allowed to search for evidence that the arrested person might destroy. While the authority to search was automatic after an arrest, it was not without reasons.

The problem with the searches in these two cases is that none of the reasons applies. Whether or not it is a reasonable constitutional premise that any person arrested

[9] By Lloyd L. Weinreb, professor at Harvard Law School.

for a substantial crime may be armed, it is certainly not a normal assumption that someone arrested for a traffic offense, even a serious traffic offense, will be armed; nor do we generally assume that persons arrested for a traffic offense will try to escape (and we do not worry about it too much if a traffic offender does "get away"). Obviously there is no evidence of the offense of driving without a license that the person might destroy. What these cases seem to say, then, is that once a person is arrested for a traffic offense, he can be searched—solely because he was arrested.

Losing Fourth Amendment Rights

The court declared bluntly that "it is the fact of the lawful arrest which establishes the authority to search." In a concurring opinion, Mr. Justice Powell emphasized that once a person is arrested his interest in privacy that the Fourth Amendment protects is gone. But it is simply silly to insist that if a man's freedom of movement is temporarily gone, he doesn't have anything more to lose by a thorough search of his pockets, his wallet, and presumably anything else he is carrying on his person.

In both cases, the court spoke of a "custodial arrest," so the decisions do not necessarily cover the multitude of situations in which one of us commits a traffic offense, is ticketed, and goes on his way. But so long as the offense is one for which we *could* be taken into custody, *either* the court has set us up for the argument that since the police officer *could* make a custodial arrest he should be allowed to search, *or* the court has set us up to be arrested custodially *in fact* because the officer wants to search, when otherwise we might only have been ticketed.

While a police officer almost certainly could not make a custodial arrest for a trivial offense like parking overtime, the laws of many states allow an officer to require someone who commits a moving traffic offense like speeding to accompany him to the police station. Many of us who

have been caught committing such an offense find the incident a great irritation but that is all. How different it
will be if we are searched thoroughly and then taken to
the station or just searched thoroughly before being ticketed!

What is perhaps most disheartening about the decisions
is that they limit our rights without increasing our security. It serves no one, not even the police, to promote
searches in situations that involve only a traffic offense.
Stopping a motorist who gives any evidence of dangerousness, the police have not up to now hesitated to protect
themselves. Now, by their own act, they may sometimes
escalate a minor situation and make it dangerous, not only
for the person arrested, but for the police themselves.

The Supreme Court's declarations about what the Constitution permits are not, of course, instructions to the
states about what they should provide. A wise state or mu-
nicipality or a wise chief of police would instruct the police not to make searches of the kind allowed in these cases
unless there were reasons to do so other than curiosity to
see what evidence might turn up. But in the prevailing
atmosphere in this country, it is unlikely that such instructions will be given.

III. THE ROLE OF THE FBI AND THE CIA

EDITOR'S INTRODUCTION

Centering on the Federal Bureau of Investigation and the Central Intelligence Agency, the articles in this section deal with recent revelations about the unauthorized activities of these agencies.

The section opens on the FBI's long-term investigation of the Socialist Workers party discussed in an article by John M. Crewdson of the New York *Times*. This is followed by extracts from the Rockefeller CIA report by Richard L. Strout, of *The Christian Science Monitor*. Then, Frank J. Donner, of Yale Law School, presents "Memos to the Chairmen" investigating intelligence agencies.

Two articles follow on the supervision and control of the FBI and the CIA: the first is by Irving Louis Horowitz, editor of *Society* magazine; the second, by the historian Arthur Schlesinger Jr.

In the concluding article, a pseudonymous journalist offers a general defense of the illegal activities engaged in by the CIA.

AN FBI CASE HISTORY [1]

The Federal Bureau of Investigation continued to employ at least one of the techniques that characterized a controversial counterintelligence operation for at least two and a half years after April 1971, the date the bureau gave for formally terminating the program, according to previously classified documents made public . . . [on October 5, 1975].

[1] From "F.B.I. Checking of Radicals Went On Beyond Deadline," by John M. Crewdson, staff correspondent. New York *Times*. p 1+. O. 6, '75. © 1975 by The New York Times Company. Reprinted by permission.

The documents, obtained through a lawsuit against the bureau by the Socialist Workers party, which made them available, show that FBI agents visited some thirty party members or associates from April 1971 to December 1973 to tell them of the bureau's knowledge of their political affiliations and to seek information about their activities.

In four related instances described in the FBI documents, agents telephoned members of the party or its youth affiliate, the Young Socialist Alliance, and utilized what the documents termed "a jury-duty pretext" to gain information about their marital status, employment, place of birth and the like.

First Documentary Proof

The bureau practice of interviewing or contacting members of radical political organizations was mentioned in a report on the controversial program, called COINTEL-PRO, that was released by the Justice Department . . . [in November 1974]. It was one of a dozen activities making up the COINTELPRO effort.

COINTELPRO, an FBI acronym for counterintelligence program, included at least twelve efforts aimed at disrupting the activities of right- and left-wing domestic political organizations from 1956 to 1971, when the operation was formally terminated by J. Edgar Hoover, the late FBI director.

The Socialist Workers party and some individuals, including some former FBI informants, have previously alleged that the FBI continued many of the counterintelligence operations of COINTELPRO after the 1971 cutoff date, but the bureau documents released . . . [on October 5] are the first evidence made public to support the assertion.

Some of the twenty-eight persons approached directly by the FBI about their Socialist affiliation, the documents show, voluntarily provided information about themselves and their activities. Others declined to be interviewed.

In each case a record was made of the visit, and the resulting FBI files contained such information as the observations that one woman, who spoke freely, had "chain-smoked" a certain brand of cigarettes, and that a more recalcitrant young man "was wearing, at the time of contact, a T-shirt on which appeared the words *Vote Socialist party.*

Some of the reports of interviews were uncaptioned, and others were headed Security Matter. None gave any indication that the subjects were suspected of involvement in violent or otherwise criminal activities, or had been questioned for any reason other than their political affiliation.

In response to a government interrogatory issued in connection with its lawsuit, which is seeking $27 million in damages for alleged official harassment by the FBI, the party has asserted that it is a legal, nonviolent organization that seeks to elect its candidates to public office.

The Justice Department's report on COINTELPRO contained few specific details of its elements, and so most of what is now known about the fifteen-year program has been made public as a result of the party suit, the only such action filed thus far by a group that was a COINTELPRO target.

The latest group of documents also detailed a plan in 1965 by the FBI's Detroit field office to send a fictitious letter, purporting to be from a student at Wayne State University there, to the Democratic State Central Committee in Michigan alleging that a campus Democratic club had been infiltrated by the Young Socialist Alliance.

Bogus Letter Approved

Officials of FBI headquarters . . . [in Washington, D.C.], the documents showed, approved the proposal to mail the bogus letter, along with several clippings from the campus newspaper regarding the matter, to the central committee and six other state and local Democratic party organizations.

Also in 1965, the documents show, the Cleveland FBI office undertook another COINTELPRO operation that it said had led to the discharge of a public school music teacher there because she was married to Rod Holt, an Ohio official of the Socialist Workers party.

The Cleveland FBI office said in a message to FBI headquarters that while neither Mrs. Holt nor her husband was affiliated with the Communist party, the Socialist Workers party and its youth group were "a form of Communist organization" thus the Cleveland agents said they wished to take action against Mrs. Holt "since Communist-oriented teachers are in such a critical position of influence."

FBI officials here authorized the Cleveland office to inform Cleveland school officials, "on a strictly confidential basis" of Mr. Holt's political connections. Four months later the Cleveland office reported back that, "as a direct result" of its action, the Board of Education had not renewed Mrs. Holt's teaching contract.

Poem Used in Scheme

In 1963 the documents further show FBI agents in Milwaukee asked the bureau's headquarters for permission to disseminate a "poem" deriding a local Communist party organizer to party followers there.

The Milwaukee agents pointed out that a Socialist Workers official in the area was "well known for his ability to write poetry," and they expressed the hope that Communist party members who received the FBI poem would believe that the Socialist Workers poet had written it.

The proposed doggerel ran, "there was an old radical [name deleted]/ Who swapped his soapbox for a bed./ He lives in the past,/ drinks beer to the last,/ And from militant action has fled."

The target of the "poem," the agents pointed out, was "an excessive beer drinker who now shuns party work." . . . The FBI headquarters, approved the use of the verse, and asked that it be informed "of any tangible results."

The Milwaukee office replied later that "the poem has apparently met with some success," and that Communist officials in Wisconsin had concluded that the mailing of the verse was an effort by the Socialist Workers to create dissension in their ranks.

THE ROCKEFELLER CIA REPORT [2]

The 299-page Rockefeller report on the domestic activities of the CIA covers the turbulent antiwar, civil-rights era from Eisenhower to Nixon. It ranges from a harsh denunciation of President Nixon's efforts to use surveillance materials "for the President's personal political ends" to a categorical denial of charges that the CIA had any part in the assassination of President Kennedy.

The four-part, 19-chapter, 100,000-word report reviews relevant facts of the twenty-eight-year-old CIA's involvement in domestic matters, into which, the Rockefeller commission finds, it was sucked to a "minor" degree by Watergate and by the stress of the times, contrary to its specific charter.

The commission makes thirty specific recommendations to avoid such developments in the future.

Separated from text by large print are Recommendations as well as a series of Conclusions. This section says, "a detailed analysis of the facts has convinced the commission that the great majority of the CIA's domestic activities comply with its statutory authority."

The report as published June 10 at no point goes into the most controversial current issue, the role of the CIA in alleged attempts to murder foreign leaders. "Time did not permit a full investigation" of this field, the report says.

President Ford created the eight-member commission on January 4, 1975, with Vice President Nelson A. Rockefeller chairman, and David W. Belin executive director.

[2] From "Extracts from the Rockefeller CIA Report," by Richard L. Strout, staff correspondent, Washington, D.C. *Christian Science Monitor*. p 26. Je. 11, '75. Reprinted by permission from *The Christian Science Monitor* © 1975 The Christian Science Publishing Society. All rights reserved.

"The President should recommend to Congress the establishment of a joint committee on intelligence to assume the oversight role currently played by the Armed Services committees," the commission says.

Other recommendations in this field: Congress should consider making the CIA budget "at least to some extent" public; the President's Foreign Intelligence Advisory Board should be expanded to include oversight of the CIA; and the Justice Department and the CIA "should establish written guidelines for the handling of reports of criminal violations by employees of the agency or relating to its affairs."

The Commission's Salient Findings

Summarizing the report in an initial chapter, the commission includes salient findings:

☐ In 1952 the CIA began a program of surveying mail and in the final year of the program (1973) the New York office examined the outside of 2.3 million items to and from the Soviet Union, photographed 33,000 envelopes, and opened 8,700.

☐ CIA established a special operations group in August 1967, Operation CHAOS, "to collect information on dissident Americans from the CIA field stations overseas and from the FBI." In six years' operation it compiled 13,000 files involving 72,000 American citizens with documents including the computerized names of 300,000.

☐ The CIA participated in a program, February 1967-December 1968, to monitor and infiltrate dissident groups.

☐ "The investigation disclosed the domestic use of 32 wire taps, the last in 1965; 32 instances of bugging, the last in 1968; and 12 break-ins, the last in 1971. None of these was conducted under a judicial warrant and only one with the written approval of the attorney general."

☐ Involvement in "improper activities for the White House" which included notorious cases like the illegal entry into the office of Daniel Ellsberg's psychiatrist, operations of Watergate figure E. Howard Hunt, possible destruction of files in the Watergate episode, and pressure from President Nixon to reveal files "to serve the President's personal political ends."

☐ The CIA formerly operated proprietary companies as "covers," but this is reduced now to "a complex of financial companies."

☐ At one time in 1953 the CIA tested hallucinatory (LSD) drugs on humans who were not told of the tests: "One person died in 1953, apparently as a result."

☐ The CIA has "indexed some 7 million names of all nationalities; an estimated 115,000 of these are believed to be American citizens."

The Huston Plan

A striking feature of the report is its version of the June 1970 proposal of President Nixon of what came to be known as the Huston plan after Tom Charles Huston, a White House assistant, to coordinate and evaluate all forms of domestic intelligence in an interagency body. Excerpts follow:

In late February 1970, J. Edgar Hoover forbade the Bureau to engage in anything but formal, written liaison with the CIA, because CIA director Richard Helms had refused to compel a CIA officer to disclose to Hoover the name of an FBI agent who had given the officer certain FBI information late in 1969.

President Richard M. Nixon called a meeting at the White House on June 5, 1970, of the directors and officers from four of the major components of the intelligence community. . . . Four days later, on June 9, 1970, the Interagency Committee on Intelligence (ad hoc) (ICI) held its first meeting. . . .

Huston made it clear at the initial ICI meeting that President Nixon wanted the committee to assume that all methods of gathering intelligence were valid. The President, Huston said, wanted the committee, in reviewing matters which "obstructed" intelligence gathering, to consider that "everything is valid, everything is possible." All restrictions on methods were to be listed, according to Huston, so that the President could make a final decision on which methods would be employed. . . . The enumerated methods which were subject to "restraints" included electronic surveillance, mail coverage, surreptitious entry, and development of campus sources. Covert mail coverage and surreptitious entry were specifically described as illegal. . . .

On July 9, 1970, Huston advised director Helms that all communications to the White House on domestic intelligence or internal security matters were thereafter to be addressed to Huston's exclusive attention. At approximately the same time, Huston recommended to the President, through chief of staff H. R. Haldeman, that almost all the restraints on methods of intelligence collection discussed in the ICI's special report should be relaxed. Haldeman advised Huston on July 14, 1970, that the President had approved Huston's recommendations. . . .

Apparently Attorney General John Mitchell was not aware of the June 5, 1970 meeting between the President and the heads of the intelligence community or of the course of meetings and events leading up to the President's decision and direction on the Huston plan. Mr. Mitchell told Helms on July 27, 1970, that he had not heard of the Huston plan until earlier that same day, when Hoover had complained to him about Huston's July 23 memorandum. In a memorandum he made of their meeting, Helms said Mitchell had been "frank" in stating that no action should be taken on Huston's directive until Mitchell had spoken with the President. Subsequently, Mitchell expressed his opposition to the Huston plan, apparently with success. The next day, July 28, the White House asked Helms to return his copy of Huston's July 23 memorandum. Soon thereafter, in late August or early September, John Dean was assigned White House responsibility for domestic intelligence on internal security matters.

Using CIA Files for Politics

President Nixon made efforts to declassify CIA files in the midst of the Watergate scandal apparently, according to the restrained appraisal of the Rockefeller commission, to find material derogatory to the earlier Kennedy-Johnson administrations.

Excerpts from the report:

During 1971, a major effort was undertaken by the White House staff on instructions from the President to declassify documents and files of historical interest. Within the White House, the declassification campaign, although inherently legitimate, was also sought to be used for political purposes by providing materials embarrassing to critics of the Administration.

The White House staff at first, and President Nixon finally, brought pressure to bear on the CIA to turn over to the President highly sensitive materials ostensibly for legitimate government purposes, but in fact for the President's personal political ends. . . .

With the publication of the Pentagon Papers in June 1971, these activities gained added significance and urgency. While the Administration was concerned over the breach of security caused by the leak of the Pentagon Papers, it was also concerned over what it considered to be an unfairly selective disclosure of embarrassing historical data.

By declassifying additional sensitive files relating to prior events—mainly the Bay of Pigs, the Cuban missile crisis, and the fall of the Diem government in South Vietnam—it sought to obtain material helpful in neutralizing critics of the Administration's policies and particularly Senator Edward Kennedy, who in 1971 was regarded as Nixon's principal challenger. Beginning in June 1971, (aides Charles) Colson and (David) Young urged on Haldeman and Ehrlichman a campaign of disclosures embarrassing to past administrations. That program involved the use of the Pentagon Papers, as well as the declassification of other files.

On September 22, 1971, Ehrlichman met with Helms, advised him that the President wanted to declassify the documents relating to Vietnam, the Bay of Pigs, the Cuban missile crisis, and the Lebanon landings, and asked to have the CIA's files on these matters turned over to him. Helms directed an internal review of these papers to make an assessment of the impact of their possible declassification. . . .

On October 1, 1971, Ehrlichman again met with Helms at the agency. Helms showed Ehrlichman the files which he proposed to turn over in response to the earlier requests and asked that they be returned as soon as possible. He declined, however, to release the files relating to Vietnam. The other files were delivered to Ehrlichman that day.

On October 8, 1971, Helms was called to a meeting at the White House with the President and Ehrlichman, apparently because he had declined to release the Vietnam file. A contemporaneous CIA memorandum states that Nixon and Ehrlichman assured Helms that the President was interested in helping the CIA and had no intention of releasing CIA papers. . . .

Both Ehrlichman and Helms have testified that Helms was not told of the President's intention to use the information in these files for political purposes. The memorandum states that

Helms replied that he worked for only one President at a time and that any papers in his possession were at the President's disposal. He then handed the requested Vietnam file to Nixon, who slipped it into his desk drawer.

The Rockefeller commission concludes:

The White House demand for sensitive CIA files—cloaked in what appear to be at least in part false representations that they were needed for valid government purposes when, in fact, they were wanted to discredit critics of the Administration—was thoroughly reprehensible. It represents another serious instance of misuse of the agency by the White House. . . .

The most sensitive of these files was turned over by the director only upon direct request from the President.

The commission recognizes that the director cannot be expected to disobey a direct request or order from the President without being prepared to resign. The instances in which resignation may be called for cannot be specified in advance and must be left to the director's judgment.

The CIA and Watergate

The commission exonerates the CIA in the Watergate break-in. One excerpt:

The origins of Watergate go back to a program for political espionage in connection with the 1972 presidential campaign on which Hunt and Liddy began to work early that year. That program had various facets, of which espionage directed against the headquarters of the Democratic National Committee was one.

This investigation has disclosed no evidence that the agency provided support for the espionage program which culminated in the Watergate break-in.

As has been discussed, however, four of the participants in the break-in—Hunt, Martinez, Barker, and McCord—had ties to the agency. Martinez continued on the CIA payroll as an informer until after his arrest. Hunt had dealings with the agency in the summer and fall of 1973 in connection with the White House projects previously discussed. And he continued to be employed by Mullen, . . . [a public relations firm with] a CIA relationship, and to be associated with [its owner, Robert Foster] Bennett in several projects with political or espionage overtones.

(The commission details the role of each of the four men listed above and repeats its conclusion that "there is no evidence either that the CIA was a participant in the planning or execution of the Watergate break-in or that it had advance knowledge of it.")

The commission condemns CIA for failure to make timely disclosure of what it knew of Watergate to the Ervin Senate committee. After detailing this episode it concludes, in part:

The agency failed to turn over to the Department of Justice information in its possession which it should have known could be relevant to the ongoing investigation and preparation for the first Watergate trial in January 1973. Much of the information requested could have been provided with little, if any, risk to the security of agency activities. Some of it was eventually provided, but only after some delay. The agency is subject to serious criticism for this conduct.

The basis for the agency's action appears to have been the director's opinion that since the agency was not involved in Watergate, it should not become involved in the Watergate investigation. The commission considers this to be no justification for the agency's failure to aid an investigation of possible violations of law by employees or ex-employees with whom it had had recent contacts. The provision of the agency's charter barring it from exercising "police, subpoena [and] law enforcement powers" does not excuse that failure.

The commission has found no evidence, however, that leads it to believe that officers of the agency actively joined in the cover-up conspiracy formed by the White House staff in June 1972.

The commission also surveys destruction by the CIA director Richard Helms of part of his tapes and transcripts.

The commission concludes, in part:

The destruction of the tapes and transcripts, coming immediately after Senator Mansfield's request not to destroy materials bearing on the Watergate investigation, reflected poor judgment.

It cannot be justified on the ground that the agency produced its Watergate-related papers from other files; there is no way in which it can ever be established whether relevant evidence has been destroyed. When taken together with the agency's general nonresponsiveness to the ongoing investigation, it reflects a serious lack of comprehension of the obligation of any citizen to produce for investigating authorities evidence in his possession of possible relevance to criminal conduct.

The commission seeks to make plain the legitimate need of a counterintelligence and information agency in the government. A seven-page, small-type appendix includes a chronological summary of domestic turbulence, 1966-1972, as a backdrop against which the CIA operated.

INVESTIGATING INTELLIGENCE AGENCIES [3]

The following observations are set down for possible consideration by the select committees of the Senate and the House, appointed to study the intelligence activities of various agencies and branches of the government. They are also respectfully called to the attention of Vice President Rockefeller, assigned by President Ford to head an Executive panel investigating intelligence activities by US agencies.

1. The key question of course is one of power. The statute creating the CIA in 1947 is extraordinarily vague. It seems fair to say that never has a single government agency been granted so much power with so few meaningful standards and restraints. The most notable example of its vagueness is perhaps the failure to define the term *intelligence activities.* It would appear from the legislative history that Congress thought this referred exclusively to passive data collection, worlds away from the aggressive covert practices

---

[3] From "Memos to the Chairmen: The Issue, of Course, Is Power," by Frank J. Donner, director of the American Civil Liberties Union research project on political surveillance at the Yale University Law School. *Nation.* 220:200-4. F. 22, '75. Copyright 1975 in the U.S.A. by the Nation Associates, Inc. Reprinted by permission.

which subsequently became the CIA's trademark. The agency is barred, as everybody now knows, from "internal security functions." Congress intended to proscribe secret political police practices on our shores, but surely there are more precise ways of conveying this purpose. The very section which seems to bar internal security functions authorizes the director to protect "intelligence sources and methods from unauthorized disclosure." Was this proviso intended to offer an escape hatch from the prohibition to which it is attached?

2. That the CIA flouted the congressional intent is hardly open to question. *Flouted* is precisely the word. For example, after the widespread furor in the early months of 1967, in the wake of the disclosure of the CIA's Covert Action Division program of hidden subsidies to some thirty-nine American organizations over a period of seventeen years—after the admissions of impropriety and the hand wringing—the Johnson Administration *in the summer of that same year* used the CIA for domestic operations against the antiwar movement. Dean Rusk, whose memory has now become conveniently vague on the subject, regularly attacked the movement as foreign-influenced, presumably on the basis of CIA data collected by a new unit formed within its counterintelligence department "to look into the possibility of foreign links to American dissident elements." In 1970-1971 the Nixon Administration commissioned the CIA to turn up evidence of foreign influence not only on the antiwar movement but on the entire New Left and black militancy. It would not take much digging to discover that since 1967 the CIA has pursued a virtually uninterrupted course of domestic intelligence operations. This pattern is not uniform; when the FBI broke with the CIA in 1970, the operational activities of the CIA intensified in this country. A particularly rich source of local operations were the "contract" employees, especially the pro-Castro Cubans in Florida and Los Angeles. Also, there is evidence

of a chain of "proprietary fronts," businesses set up by the CIA for intelligence purposes.

A Government of Men or Laws?

3. As the statute now stands, the director of the CIA has almost unrestrained and unreviewed power to determine the nature and scope of its operations. Indeed, this vagueness in the delegation of power was deliberate: it was central to Allen Dulles' format for the new agency. The CIA's legislative warrant creates the very "government of men" which the Founders of the Republic feared. The CIA's abuses of power over the years attest to the wisdom of a "government of laws" and the dangers of entrusting decision making to the values and policies of powerful individuals, themselves captives of the mystique of intelligence.

However clumsily Congress may have originally expressed itself, it is incontestable that it did not intend to create in the CIA the autonomous power system it seems to have become. The emergence and growth of an independent organ of state administration to monitor the opinions and political activities of a country's nationals are among the hallmarks of a police state. The CIA was created to assemble and evaluate data as an aid in the formulation of policy and the making of decisions by agencies of government (the National Security Council, the State Department and the White House) charged with substantive responsibilities.

4. There is an observable pathology in the process by which intelligence agencies enlarge their powers. For more than three decades Director J. Edgar Hoover maintained that the FBI had been entrusted by a presidential directive of September 1939 with an open-ended intelligence mission unrelated to law enforcement. When Director Kelley took over in 1973, this claimed Magna Carta for domestic political intelligence was all but abandoned. Similarly, the bureau's political filing practices were justified by an invented intelligence mandate, until the Congress, by a recent statute,

required a law-enforcement justification. In the same way, despite the austere language of the Constitution limiting the Army's role in civilian affairs, military intelligence developed a vast civilian surveillance capability, wholly unrelated to its narrow mission of responding to a call-out when, in the judgment of the President, such action was warranted.

5. The reasons for expansion of domestic intelligence beyond its intended limits are evident. To begin with, intelligence operations typically become the responsibility of zealots, men who are committed to the long twilight struggle. Further, the intelligence process itself is inherently subject to abuse: one investigates in order to discover whether there is a need to investigate. Every activity of the target, however legitimate and indeed constitutionally protected, is treated with suspicion and monitored: who knows, it may be a vital piece in a sinister not-yet-revealed subversive design. Since, in the intelligence mind, the stakes are so large—our very survival as a nation—overkill is almost deliberate. Ultimately, the intelligence institution exploits reasons of state to achieve autonomy and, by a parallel process, its operations become ends in themselves. The goal of collecting information is transformed into one of doing injury to the target.

Counterintelligence Operations

6. The great *idée fixe* of the intelligence mind is that domestic protest and dissent ("agitation") are the fruits of foreign plotting and direction. Intelligence functionaries and agents in other countries are amused by the readiness of their American counterparts to justify their domestic practices as defensive, "counterintelligence." All sorts of domestic intelligence programs in this country, whatever the motivation or authority, are automatically labeled "counterintelligence." This not only avoids the stigma of affirmatively initiating a program of spying on one's own nationals but evades problems of authorization and constitutionality.

For example, in the 1972 *Keith* case the Supreme Court
ruled that domestic wiretapping for intelligence purposes
(as opposed to law enforcement) was subject to the warrant
requirements of the Fourth Amendment. The Department
of Justice, overnight, ascribed to its electronic eavesdropping a "foreign intelligence" justification which had been
excluded from the scope of the Court's decision. One can
see this form of rationalization at work in the report by the
Saxbe committee on the FBI's counterintelligence programs
(COINTELPROs). The document, released in November
1974, justifies the most aggressive instances of counterintelligence, a program conducted for some fifteen years against
nominal Communists, on the ground that it "was conceived
as a 'counterintelligence' effort in the purest sense." The
targets, the report argued, were embryonic foreign spies and
saboteurs. The other six COINTELPROs were presumably
also defensive initiatives against foreign plotters—but in
some less pure sense. [Assistant] Attorney General [Henry
E.] Petersen thought so highly of this formulation that,
when he retired . . . [from government service], he used the
report's conclusions as a warning against overreacting to
the CIA's domestic efforts. In the same way the Army's enormous computerized domestic intelligence filing operation at
Fort Holabird, with its 100,000 subjects was called the
Counterintelligence Analysis Branch, the allegation being
that it was merely monitoring the activities of foreign intelligence agents.

A supersecret FBI counterintelligence program was designated Special Operations. The full details of this program
were withheld when facts about the other counterintelligence programs were made public, on the ground that it
dealt with the intelligence activities of a hostile foreign
power. But the three documents which were released bearing the file caption of this program deal with the Black
Panthers—hardly, whatever one may say about them, the
intelligence agents of a foreign power. Similarly, campus informers and ghetto plants of the bureau were in the late

1960s and early 1970s regularly instructed to look for evidence of foreign collaboration in the activities of their targets.

7. The 1947 CIA statute simply permits other intelligence agencies to continue domestic data collection. This provision is as tricky as the "intelligence sources and methods" provision already discussed. Did this backhandedly authorize the FBI to engage in practices which are not spelled out in any other more direct mandate to the bureau? It is becoming fairly clear, although Director Kelley is not giving up without a struggle, that the FBI has no ongoing intelligence responsibilities unrelated to law enforcement, at least in the area of domestic intelligence. But the bureau still insists that it is charged with a foreign intelligence responsibility with respect to such matters as the actions of foreign agents and other domestic "subversive activities" with a foreign dimension. In this area, too, we may need corrective or clarifying legislation.

Investigating Political Activities

8. The domestic investigation of political activities by the bureau has been justified either on law-enforcement or intelligence grounds. The Nixon Administration developed the thesis that political investigations for intelligence purposes could be more intrusive and hostile to constitutional rights than could an investigation for purposes of law enforcement. This position emerged from the cold war, but Attorney General Mitchell elevated it to the level of a principle. Under this formulation a bomb-laden terrorist under criminal investigation could not be made the subject of a wiretap without the protection of the warrant procedures of Title III of the 1968 law. But an individual merely suspected of "subversive activities" could be electronically monitored with no concern for his rights. There is one case described in an affidavit submitted by Attorney General Saxbe in a lawsuit (March 18, 1974) of a wiretap which was commenced on October 24, 1942, and not discontinued

until February 10, 1967. This marathon surveillance was targeted against "an organization whose activities were controlled" by another organization composed of citizens of the United States but, according to the affidavit, dominated by an organization acting on behalf of a foreign power. Bear in mind that for twenty-five years all of this target's outgoing and incoming calls to and from whatever party were recorded, logged and filed. What intelligence purpose was served by such a massive invasion of both privacy and free expression? [For another view of this matter, see "A Favorable Word for the CIA," the concluding article in this Section.—Ed.]

9. There is an understandable fear that members of Congress have been made special targets of surveillance and filing practices. But the answer to this well-documented abuse is certainly not to immunize legislators, *ex officio,* as it were, from FBI investigation. The nation was shocked when evidence emerged that Acting Director L. Patrick Gray III protected the Nixon Administration from the bureau's Watergate investigation. It will not do to shelter members of Congress from legitimate bureau investigations. What is imperatively needed is a precise formulation of the bureau's investigative jurisdiction, of its authority for *all* data collection. A recent case in point demonstrates the necessity. After the director retreated from the claim that his bureau had an ongoing intelligence jurisdiction unrelated to law enforcement, he continued his former practices but simply changed the justification. Although the Young Socialist Alliance [YSA] had programmatically rejected violence and, indeed, expelled advocates of violence, the bureau justified infiltrating its convention in December 1974 on the ground that the YSA might conceivably, at some future time, engage in criminal violence and that the bureau's law-enforcement responsibilities required such infiltration as a preventive measure. Not only were rights of the convention attendants violated but the courts were deceived by this strained interpretation.

10. It will be quite difficult, if not impossible, to impose meaningful positive standards on the operations of an intelligence agency. A far more realistic course would be to state in unequivocal language what an agency may not do. Senator Ervin introduced such a measure, barring the military from the civilian surveillance area, but it died in the . . . [93d] Congress.

Quarantining Forbidden Areas

11. A precisely worded quarantine of forbidden areas and practices is imperative for another reason. Every intelligence agency rapidly substitutes for its mandate a "mission." The mission, a key intelligence concept, is a grandiose, ideologized reinterpretation by the agency of its responsibilities; it leads both to abuse of power and to competition with other agencies.

12. The CIA is a member of an intelligence community in the fields of both foreign and domestic intelligence. Especially over the past decade, surveillance operations, the development and storage of files and dossiers, have become a collaborative endeavor by a constellation of federal, state and urban agencies. An agency that is barred by its mandate or lack of funds from a particular area of domestic intelligence enters into a liaison relationship with other units with a similar or overlapping mission for the purpose of exchanging data, operational information and files. Liaison relationships are not casual or optional aspects of intelligence but functional. (This happens all over the world; the British describe it by the verb *to liaise.*) Thus, when intelligence agencies are not cutting each other's throats in the competition for funding and power, they are borrowing each other's capability to accomplish indirectly what they are barred from doing directly.

13. The congressional mandate authorizes the select committees to explore the need for "improved, strengthened or consolidated oversight" of domestic intelligence activities. This problem should have top priority. Neither the existing oversight panels nor the President's commission can effectively probe the abuses of the CIA and its sister agencies in the domestic field. The precedent for Executive oversight is President Johnson's three-man committee headed by Under Secretary of State Nicholas DeB. Katzenbach, which took less than six weeks to return its emollient conclusions. The pattern of legislative response when the CIA comes under attack has been marked by a curious protectiveness. The committee chairman summons the elders of the agency and accepts their justification for its conduct. There is no real will to get at the facts. One is reminded of the tear-stained boy who pleaded with Shoeless Joe Jackson at the time of the Black Sox scandals to "Say it ain't so, Joe." But it is time for Congress to come to terms with fundamentals: given a residual ambiguity even in a well-drafted statute, the power of the director, the secrecy of the operation and the ease with which oversight committees are coopted, abuses are inevitable and, indeed, will increase. The intelligence functionaries know that in a democracy storms of criticism periodically strike their sanctuaries. The trick is to hibernate, to confess error, but to survive until the climate changes.

What of CIA's Domestic Surveillance?

14. The Watergate and military intelligence investigations, both directed by Senator Ervin, show that Congress can do an effective job of getting at the roots of sensitive and factually complicated problems. But fruitful investigation requires careful preparation and a competent staff. An intelligence agency operating in a politically sensitive area makes certain of its cover in advance, a claim to authorization if the operation is blown—in Malcolm Muggeridge's words, "like those iron staircases in case of fire that one sees outside brownstone houses in New York." While it may not have taken much to activate the CIA's domestic surveillance, the agency almost certainly received a signal from some higher authority—not in writing, of course, but in some form. In fact, the evidence is clear that every Administration since that of Eisenhower has either authorized or ratified CIA domestic intelligence operations.

15. The investigation of domestic intelligence practices is child's play compared to a probe of the CIA's covert actions abroad, and there is a particular reason why the two areas should be studied in separate stages of any investigation. The committees should strive to make public as much information as is possible without compromising matters which have a colorable claim to secrecy. It would be unfortunate if foreign-related considerations were used to screen from public view information about domestic activities which have no valid claim to secrecy. Yet, if the past is a guide, the danger of such a cover-up is great.

16. Finally, there is no point even starting without planning to call the insiders, the kinds of people who have contributed to the success of every important congressional investigation. The committees need to hear testimony from agency staffers, whether now employed or retired. But they must evaluate the testimony, from whatever source, in the light of today's world. A vast intelligence bureaucracy, rooted in the needs and assumptions of the 1940s, is threatened by heaving historic changes—not only in the world political situation but in the very techniques of data collection. The persons involved will go to great lengths to conform reality to their ideological biases and occupational needs. What legitimate governmental purpose should intelligence, both domestic and foreign, serve? A sound answer to that question will give needed perspective to the problems of authority, coordination, operations and data evaluation.

In a post-Watergate America theories of inherent Executive power can no longer serve to justify secret intelligence baronies either at home or abroad. But does Congress have the will and resources to forge a legitimate alternative?

DEALING WITH THE CIA AND THE FBI [4]

Those fellows in the CIA don't just report on wars and the like, they go out and make their own, and there's nobody to keep track of what they are up to. They spend billions of dollars on stirring up trouble so they'll have something to report on. They've become . . . it's become a government all of its own and all secret. They don't have to account to anybody.

The author of these words, the late President of the United States, Harry S. Truman, speaks with a special authority on this subject—he was responsible as President for setting up the CIA (cf. *Plain Speaking: An Oral Biography of Harry S. Truman,* by Merle Miller).

The thin line between intelligence and surveillance, between the public's right to know and the citizen's right to privacy, is the foundation of much current American soul searching. Both principles, the right to knowledge and the right to privacy, are firmly entrenched in the constitutional tradition. Thus, the existence of investigatory agencies are troublesome to the extent that they involve us in a legal double-bind—a veritable contradiction between competing needs in a modern society. The limits of privacy come full force against the limits of knowledge. And choices are made in terms of shifts in the moral sentiment more than new legal foundations of the social order.

But in American social history issues of ideology are fought out and masked by contrasting administrative claims. This was made virtually certain given the fact that the American polity derives from Montesquieu's legal premises that shared power prevents its undue exercise. Thus, the legislative branch stands in the forefront of those demanding the right to know about the entire gamut of CIA activities; arguing in effect that the agency is ultimately re-

[4] Revised version of "Spying and Security: The American Way," by Irving Louis Horowitz, editor-in-chief of *Society* magazine. *Society.* 12:7-10. Mr./Ap. '75. Published by permission of Transaction, Inc. Copyright © 1975, by Transaction, Inc. Revised version supplied by author.

sponsive to Congress since it alone is the repository of the
popular will. The executive branch is obviously reluctant
to pursue such a line of reasoning; its growth in powers
since the end of the Second World War clearly derives
from the secrecy implicit in a policy-making (in contrast to
a polity-making) approach. The steady stream of publications issuing forth from hearings and testimonies held by
both branches of Congress are a firm indicator that the right
of the public to all agency activities is about the only mech-
anism available to prevent yet a further erosion of legislative powers and their transfer to executive branches. Thus,
politically, no less than ideologically, the current revalua-
tion of CIA activities involves principles of a fundamental
sort—the sort that ultimately might redefine who governs
and beyond that, the limits of governance.

The Federal Bureau of Investigation and the Central
Intelligence Agency have been with us for quite some time.
Their activities are hardly esoteric or mysterious. So the
question becomes why has the role of intelligence-gathering
agencies and federal police-bureaus come under widespread
critical examination at this point in our national history?

The answers are obviously complex and multiple: the
dismay and disgust of the public with the Watergate
break-in and its aftermath, and the obvious collusion of
party officials with federal agencies in first creating a po-
lice-state climate, and second, in suppressing the full story.
Then there is a general mistrust of federal bureaucracy, a
realization that the need to know has spilled over into a
desire to dominate—a far less noble purpose; and the sense
that the only way to restore confidence in government is
to expose the illegitimate behavior of those who transgress
the legitimate boundaries of government. Finally, there is
international pressure, from Latin America to Asia, to
curb the overseas operations of intelligence-gathering units
that in fact act as counterguerrilla units beyond the boundaries of national sovereignty.

For the most part, discussions about the CIA, and other

information-gathering agencies that spin off into action roles, confuse the moral purposes of such activities and their empirical efficacy. It is one thing to express a sense of rage about CIA spying activities on American citizens or foreign governments, and quite another to demonstrate the degree of success such activities have achieved. In these murkier waters, one does find countervailing forces at work —not only civil libertarians versus civil disrupters, but competition between agencies such as the FBI and the CIA which itself muffles, if not quite mitigates, spying activities.

In my opinion, we must combine the best of critical social science and investigative reporting to express a sense of the system as well as outrage. The restoration of international law, the new resolve toward congressional inquiry and control, the distinction between democratic restraint and antidemocratic opposition, the further distinction between the national interest and narrow commercial or military interests, all indicate ways in which government can better serve its citizenry. Spying is not, strictly speaking, an American preserve, nor is the illegal use of surveillance personnel to harass a native citizenry an American monopoly. However, it is of little worth to cite instances of terror and police spying abroad, or for that matter, historical illustrations of this phenomenon. The purpose of democratic government is normative and not simply comparative. The recitation of transgressions elsewhere, on the fatuous assumption that the role of government is more gracious and generous now than in the past eras, simply misses the point. Democracy is an ideal of equity we are collectively dedicated to achieve; it is not an equivalent of Pax Americana that must be bullishly supported wherever and whenever opposition movements, parties or systems arise.

As a result, the following seven-point minimal policy program that could and should emanate from this current round of congressional hearings and presidential commissions is indicated:

☐ A national civil liberties commission paralleling the

existing national civil rights commission should be created. This group should be appointed by Congress, should perform its duties with maximum autonomy and noninterference from other government agencies, and could function as a special ad hoc group of the Government Operations Committee of the United States Senate. The various commissions recently appointed to study CIA violations have in common a dangerous politicization; hence it is likely that nothing of consequence will result. On the side of soft-soaping CIA covert operations is the presidential commission headed by Vice President Nelson Rockefeller, and on the side of what has been called the Senate "cabal" to get the CIA is the Senate Select Investigating Committee headed by Frank Church. Most past commissions have had the benefit of social and behavioral science personnel who could file reports with meat and meaning. The present concurrent investigating commissions seem destined to generate more heat than light, and more pointedly, result in a veto effect, with the recommendations of the different commissions and subcommissions canceling out one another. What is needed is a single autonomous commission with political inputs for the Congress, the executive and the judiciary branches, but with leadership and direction provided by constitutional lawyers and political scientists.

☐ The jurisdictional disputes between agencies such as the CIA and the FBI should be brought out into the open to determine if either agency has assumed greater police roles than constitutionally warranted. Beyond that, specialized subagencies, like the passport division of the State Department should be explicitly prohibited from making special arrangements and deals with the CIA that could lead to the creation of special files for surveillance purposes, and blacklists that might inhibit citizens engaged in private activities of tourism or commerce.

☐ The CIA should limit its intelligence-gathering operations generally. At the optimal level, it does little more than repeat data and information found in social and political science, often naively, and without the balance manifested in scholarly research. CIA sponsorship of research, often having little or nothing to do with threats to American interests, only conservatizes scholarship and inhibits open exchange of information.

☐ A definition of the intelligence-gathering functions of the CIA must be established that is not so broad and diffuse as to permit the funding of conduits in areas ranging from broadcasting to publishing to student associations. It is always possible to justify and rationalize sub-rosa activities in the name of intelligence, when in point of fact the underwriting of otherwise legitimate expressions of communication for propaganda purposes serves only to discredit honest operations, and to cast grave doubts on the CIA's integrity by its uniform alignment with right-wing and conservative enterprises and causes that might otherwise be unable to survive. The CIA is entitled to support research and to publish results. But it should be made by statute to declare such support openly, and wherever possible, publish its results in official government documentation centers, rather than in privately endowed firms.

☐ Diplomacy, not counterinsurgency, should dominate in policy making abroad. The ambassadorial functions should be greatly strengthened, so that spying and surveillance activities do not take place independent of State Department control, to the embarrassment of United States foreign policy. From India to Chile, normal relations with the United States have been strained as a result of CIA secrecy, and beyond that, the avoidance of diplomatic channels assigned to foreign countries. This recommendation to move cautiously in setting up new intelligence-gathering units and to rely instead upon existing agencies was made as early as February 1947 by General George P. Marshall [then Secretary of State] in a memorandum to . . . President [Truman].

The Foreign Service of the Department of State is the only collection agency of the government which covers the whole world, and we should be very slow to subject the collection and evaluation of this foreign intelligence to other establishments, especially during times of peace. The powers of the proposed agency seem almost unlimited and need clarification.

☐ The fiscal cover under which the CIA has been permitted to operate should finally be lifted. The General Accounting Office and the citizenry have a right to demand the same public disclosure of the amount, distribution and allocation of funding as is expected of any other federal agency. Indeed, the FBI is subject to a far greater auditing responsibility than the CIA, and yet manages to carry out its assignments without jeopardy. The risks to specific assignments are virtually nonexistent. But the risks to continuing constitutional violations are great in the present atmosphere of fiscal secrecy.

☐ The major question is not simply the illegal "domestic" spying activities of the CIA, but whether its overseas activities should be restricted to information gathering rather than manifest support of conservative regimes and fomenting opposition to radical regimes. A simple rule in this connection is to have the CIA do unto other governments as they do to us. That is to say, since the Soviet Union engages in large-scale and illegal spying activities, the activities of the CIA inside the Soviet Union should be commensurate with that nation's acts inside the United States. But for nations such as Uruguay or Pakistan, who have neither the capacity nor interest in conducting spying missions in the United States, the same rules should apply to United States behavior inside those Third World nations. Real opposition to CIA activities inside other major world powers is clearly not under dispute; but rather its activities against small and relatively defenseless countries whose rights to select and implement policies are seriously undermined by CIA interference and involvement.

These seven items are not intended to provide a definitive list of suggested policy changes in the conduct of American surveillance activities, but they are aimed at moving us beyond the moral torpor which has seemingly gripped our political leadership since the Vietnam war began in earnest a decade ago, and also beyond the political infantilism of dismantling the intelligence effort unilaterally and without regard to actual world conditions.

What the various executive and legislative hearings on the CIA are likely to demonstrate are only a cluster of confirmations about atrocities already reported: assassination attempts against Left and Right leaders hostile to presumed American overseas interests, stimulating political crisis by supporting oppositionist groupings, and cloak and dagger code-breaking and gun-slinging operations having more technological than political meaning. Some exact details might prove titillating or intriguing, but none are likely to cause any fundamental reestimation of the CIA's potential for damage.

What then does the current animus and revulsion for the CIA signify? The most obvious explanation is also the most likely. From 1964 to 1974, the American people underwent a gradual but authentic change in its sense of national priorities. Economy, ecology, and environment, the three national E's displaced militarization, modernization and mobilization, the three international M's. And as the stalemated situation of the fifties led to the military defeats of the late sixties, attitudes toward redirecting our priorities hardened. Defeat has had a sobering effect on the American public; and if it would be a mistake to judge the mood of America as isolationist, it would be folly to believe that internationalist sentiments have remained firm. Even a minimal, nonmilitary task force stationed in the Middle East has come upon severe critical public reaction. The line between internationalism and imperialism has become thin—made more so by the incessant rhetoric of nationalism pouring forth from Third World nations that have been the recipients of unwanted CIA "favors."

Thus it is that the demise of the CIA is far less a function of its own bunglings and failures, than a shifting mood of Americans. A vanguard police force is less urgently needed in a period of national retrenchment than in a period of world war and cold war involvement. Thus it is that the CIA is a victim of international pacification. It is not the atrocities and bigotries it has committed in the name of American foreign policy that should be glossed over or laundered, but simply a time to recognize that all organizations—secret as well as public—are subject to the iron law of public purpose even more than to an iron law of private survival.

HOW TO CONTROL THE CIA [5]

The Central Intelligence Agency is in trouble, and for good reason. No one argues against the idea of an agency for the collection and analysis of foreign intelligence. But there is increasing evidence that the CIA has been an agency out of control and increasing doubt about the "dirty tricks" approach to international relations, especially in view of the fact that the agency has played its dirty tricks on the American people too.

The CIA developed its clandestine skills in the early Cold War—espionage, in order to improve the quality of intelligence about foreign states; counterintelligence, in order to protect American agents and secrets abroad from adversary intelligence services; and covert action, a vague category which the Murphy Commission has recently defined as "activity abroad intended not to gather information but to influence events." [Robert D. Murphy, former career diplomat, was chairman of the Commission on the Organization of Government for the Conduct of Foreign Policy, which made its final report July 1, 1975.—Ed.] These skills were employed by the branch of CIA now known as the Directorate for Operations and were aimed at Stalin and his em-

[5] From "What About the CIA?" by Arthur Schlesinger Jr., Albert Schweitzer Professor of the Humanities at the City University of New York, winner of Pulitzer Prizes in history and biography. *Wall Street Journal.* p 8. Jl. 2, '75. Reprinted with permission of *The Wall Street Journal.* © 1975 Dow Jones & Company, Inc. All Rights Reserved.

pire. They had the support—in principle if not in detail—of Congress and public opinion.

Covert action—the so-called "department of dirty tricks" —began mildly enough with assistance to democratic parties, trade unions, newspapers and so on in Western Europe in the early years of the Marshall Plan, when the Soviet Union was pouring in subsidies to Communist organizations. In the fifties covert action grew more ambitious and aggressive. It set itself not just to support our friends but to do in our foes. The CIA helped overthrow regimes in Iran and Guatemala, tried to overthrow the regime in Indonesia, prepared to overthrow the regime in Cuba. In these heady years the covert action operators acquired paramilitary delusions, established private armies and air forces and toward the end evidently began to interpret their mission as including the murder of foreign leaders.

The world meanwhile began to change. Stalin died. Nationalism shattered the unity of his empire. The prospect of nuclear holocaust produced a movement toward detente. But the Directorate for Operations did not change. It still represented the institutionalization of the early Cold War. Long after the emergencies that had led the CIA into covert action began to recede, the operators, propelled by the mood and momentum of another time, kept on coming up with elaborate and increasingly mischievous projects.

It may be argued that the costs of covert action began to exceed the benefits as soon as we moved on from the support of our friends to the subversion of our foes. Those great CIA "triumphs" of the fifties—installing the Shah in Iran, turning out a left-wing regime in Guatemala—hardly seem in the retrospect of twenty years to have advanced the national interest all that much. But the impression of the United States created by CIA intervention around the globe has damaged us very clearly and gravely.

A dozen years ago Harry Truman wrote, "There is something about the way the CIA has been functioning that is casting a shadow over our historic position." He went on to recommend that CIA "be restored to its original assignment as the intelligence arm of the President . . . and that its operational duties be terminated."

This in effect is what Congress tried to do . . . [in 1974] in the Hughes Amendment to the Foreign Assistance Act. That amendment prohibits the use of CIA funds "for operations in foreign countries, other than intelligence activities intended solely for obtaining necessary intelligence" unless the President determines that the operation is "important to the national security" and reports it to the House and Senate foreign relations committees. The Hughes Amendment should effectively end large-scale covert adventures.

But it is not so easy to eliminate less noisy forms of influence and intervention. Take South Vietnam in 1963. A CIA officer was in contact with the anti-Diem generals solely for intelligence purposes. Yet his presence in their councils undoubtedly encouraged the generals to carry out their coup. The CIA may bribe an official of a foreign government in order to gather information. But what is the case officer to do if the bribed official asks what position to take on a policy issue within his government?

Internal and External Controls Needed

Such ambiguities make it clear that control—internal and external—is the essence of the problem. But the CIA by nature is an organization difficult to control. It is vast, self-contained, meticulously compartmentalized, saturated with the religion of secrecy. The idea of restricting information to those with a "need to know" has often meant that the right hand had no notion what the left was doing. The Intelligence branch, for example, was never told about the Bay of Pigs operation, though its estimate of the probable reaction of the Cuban people might have been exceedingly instructive. Nor indeed were the men running that operation in Washington aware of the assurances their case officers in the field were giving the exiles about American military support.

"Even persons whose function it is to oversee or inspect CIA activities," the Rockefeller Commission tells us, "are sometimes denied complete access to operational details." The CIA Inspector General "was sometimes refused access to particularly sensitive CIA activities." The CIA program of administering LSD to unsuspecting subjects, one of whom killed himself, started in 1953; the Inspector General did not learn about it until 1963. The CIA program directed against dissenters in the United States was "not effectively supervised and reviewed by anyone in the CIA who was not operationally involved in it." In over half the records of CIA wiretaps, bugs and unauthorized entries, "a clear showing of the authorizing official is missing." The Rockefeller Commission's portrait is of an agency singularly defective in its mechanisms of internal control.

Nor has external control been any more effective. Vice President Rockefeller remarked . . . "It's fair to say that no major undertakings were taken by the CIA without either knowledge and-or approval of the White House." The Vice President ought to read his own report. Five percent of that report is devoted to CIA's mail intercept activities, which ran from 1953 to 1973 and which have been accurately described by Morton Halperin as "the largest, clearly illegal and unconstitutional programs discovered by the commission." Four men served as President in these years; but "no evidence could be found"—so Rockefeller's own commission testifies—"that any briefing of any President occurred."

The CIA and Assassinations

All this may provide a clue to the assassination business. It now seems plain that in 1960 some people in CIA enlisted gangsters in a plot to kill Castro. This must have been proposed in connection with the idea of an exile invasion of Cuba. Killing Castro in a vacuum would only have meant his replacement by his brother Raul or by Che Guevara;

killing him in the context of the invasion might have been thought a means of assuring the invasion's success.

In any case the assassination plot was incontestably conceived in the Eisenhower Administration. Did Rockefeller mean to imply . . . that this very major undertaking had the knowledge and-or approval of the Eisenhower White House? Assassination sounds out of character for Eisenhower, as for Kennedy. Maybe the Church Committee should ask the then Vice President about the Castro plot. For no one in the Eisenhower White House was more involved in the Bay of Pigs project than Richard Nixon, who later described himself as "the strongest and most persistent advocate for setting up and supporting such a program."

The assassination element was later either glossed over or dropped out. As one who sat through the top secret White House meetings before the Bay of Pigs, I can testify that no one there talked about murdering Castro. Perhaps the CIA did not wish the new White House to know about its alliance with the Mafia. Certainly the agency retained what is called in the trade an "executive action" section, producing "plans" of a most drastic sort. But at what point did the agency think it must submit such plans for external clearance—when the plans were still on the drafting board, or after agents had already been hired and put in place, or as the attempt was under way? To what extent could Washington control its own operatives in the field? To what extent could operatives in the field control opposition groups to which aid had been supplied? There is also the question what men in the CIA, hellbent on their pet projects, took as White House clearance. People might talk around the cabinet table about "removing" or "deposing" Castro. But that could mean overthrowing his regime to one side of the table and murdering him to the other.

The essential problem is control. Control both within CIA and within the executive branch has evidently been a failure. This argues that Congress might as well enter the breach; and the Hughes Amendment ought to end the noisiest forms of covert action. More can be done. Cutting the CIA budget by, say, 50 percent would eliminate much of the cloak-and-dagger nonsense and compel the agency to concentrate on the collection and analysis of intelligence. A joint congressional committee could also help; but, though such a committee can and should review targets and priorities, it really cannot oversee the day-to-day detail of clandestine operations.

Two additional proposals, both from men with long and serious experience in this field, are worth consideration. The so-called 40 Committee is charged with the clearance of covert action. The 40 Committee consists of harried officials whose primary responsibilities lie elsewhere. There seems to me great merit in Franklin Lindsay's suggestion of a full-time review committee composed of senior persons seasoned in international relations who can think through the benefits and costs of proposed clandestine operations. [Franklin Anthony Lindsay is a corporation executive and writer on national and foreign policy.—Ed.] And there also seems great merit in Harry Rositzke's proposal of an intelligence ombudsman, appointed by and accountable to the joint congressional committee, to whom any federal employee with reason to suppose that his agency is carrying out illegal actions can turn. [Harry August Rositzke, author of *The U.S.S.R. Today* (Day, 1973), was formerly with the Office of Strategic Services and for twenty-seven years with the Central Intelligence Agency.—Ed.]

We need an effective intelligence agency, but we cannot afford an intelligence agency that acts as if it were a law unto itself.

A FAVORABLE WORD FOR THE CIA [6]

The awesome capacity of American democracy to enhance its own destruction has seldom been so exquisitely
illustrated as in the current storm over alleged "domestic
spying" by the Central Intelligence Agency.

The latest experiment in national self-flagellation was
touched off on the front page of the New York *Times* three
days before Christmas [1974], when Seymour Hersh wrote
that the CIA had mounted a "massive illegal domestic intelligence operation during the Nixon Administration
against the antiwar movement and other dissident groups."

Hersh, who won a Pulitzer Prize for uncovering the My
Lai massacre, said the CIA operation had apparently resulted in the compiling of "intelligence files" on at least
10,000 American citizens.

He reported the CIA had used wiretaps, mail inspection
and break-ins "aimed at suspected foreign intelligence
agents operating in the United States."

Both activities—against the dissidents and against the
possible foreign agents—were in violation of the CIA's
charter, which specifically prohibits the agency from "police,
subpoena, law enforcement powers or internal security functions" inside the United States, the *Times* noted.

The Hersh story relied on unnamed "sources," did not
name any of the US citizens "on file" with the CIA, and
gave no documentation or details on how the intelligence
operation was carried out.

President Gerald R. Ford called for, and got within a
few days, a report on the matter from CIA Director William
E. Colby, which apparently confirmed the essence of the
Times story. Colby had already assured the President that
such activities were not now being carried out by the agency.

[6] From "Will CIA Survive This Anti-Intelligence Mania?" by John Ligonier
(pseudonym of a Washington-based journalist). *Human Events.* p 1+. Ja. 11, '75.
Reprinted by permission.

Nonetheless, Ford felt constrained to tell reporters flocking after him on his Vail, Colorado, ski vacation that "under no circumstances would I tolerate such activities under this Administration." But by this time the Capitol Hill handwringers were already racing for the nearest television camera or microphone to vent their indignation.

Others, who might have defended the CIA, kept silent. The entire show was played in an incredible atmosphere in which no one sought to detail the potential internal and external security threats that might have motivated the agency.

As an unfortunate (from a national security standpoint) fallout from the affair, four key CIA men resigned their positions.

Seemingly lost in the hubbub was the fact that the activities in question ceased apparently before 1973. The final stroke against them was made in early 1973, when James R. Schlesinger, . . . [later] secretary of defense, took over the CIA. He ordered a halt of all "questionable" agency intelligence operations inside the United States.

Also missing from the debate was any hard information that would clarify the issue of the alleged "files," which in and of themselves would not appear to be illegal. Might not these files contain information that does indeed bear on the national security? Might they not contain information routinely "passed along" from elsewhere in the intelligence community? Is it extraordinary to suggest there might in this land of 200 million people be at least 10,000 whose names might have shown up in connection with the wide-ranging clandestine operations of foreign powers?

Perspective Needed on the 1960s

Even more importantly, neither the *Times* nor the majority of the press tried to put the "spy" charges in the harsh and necessary perspective of the turmoil and confusion being fostered by the Left in the United States during

the 1960s and on up to the present time. It is useful to recall a few facts.

First, there was a rising crescendo of increasingly violent
demonstrations against the Vietnam war, disruptions on
campuses and in Washington itself, and acts of bombing and
sabotage against military installations and public buildings.

Communist terrorist literature and operational manuals
were finding their way into the country from Third World
countries in which Soviet and Chinese Communist agents
were known to be actively operating.

Rabidly anti-American groups like the Students for a
Democratic Society (SDS) were taking on a sinister inter-
national character. As the House Committee on Internal
Security's staff study on terrorism notes:

"In accordance with [an] increasing fascination with terrorist guerrilla theory, SDS leaders began to make more
journeys to Hanoi and Havana." Some of these trips lasted
for many weeks and culminated in 1968 in a "workshop on
sabotage" at the SDS convention.

Antiwar coalitions which the American press routinely
treated as "broad-based" groups of liberals, pacifists and
"activists," were in most cases controlled by intensely vio-
lence-prone and anti-American organizations which appeared to have important international connections. Case
in point: the Trotskyite Socialist Workers party (SWP) and
its youth arm, the Young Socialist Alliance [YSA].

SWP/YSA members, who regularly attended international Trotskyite conventions such as the Fourth International, completely controlled the National Peace Action
Coalition (NPAC) which gulled thousands of "sheep" into
disruptive demonstrations all over the country.

During this period, US intelligence units had to contend
with many other groups the members of which engaged in
extensive foreign travel to countries like North Korea,
North Vietnam and Cuba.

Possible foreign influences in the travels, activities and
ideologies of these and other groups would certainly have

to be considered by any intelligence people interested in the nation's security. And it cannot be overstressed that the CIA would be in a unique position to examine these activities in the light of special information gathered by its worldwide apparatus.

For example, how should one view the international travel of activists in the light of this paragraph from a top-secret KGB [Russian secret police] manual entitled "The Practice of Recruiting Americans in the U.S.A. and Third Countries"? (Printed as an appendix in John Barron's important book *KGB: The Secret Work of Soviet Secret Agents.* Reader's Digest Press. 1974):

It is particularly important to note the expediency of bringing Americans out of the United States to third countries where the operational climate is more suitable. It is especially desirable to use the People's Democracies and in certain cases even the USSR.

The CIA Caseload

It is useful to remember, too, that the "caseload"of the FBI and other intelligence-gathering outfits was overwhelming at the time. There is evidence that, although the CIA is supposed to turn over the domestic aspects of its investigations to the FBI, cooperation between the agencies has not always been the best.

J. Edgar Hoover, then director of the FBI, is reported to have repeatedly turned down CIA requests for help on surveillance matters resulting from foreign CIA cases traced back to the United States.

It is hardly implausible to envision names building up rapidly in CIA files:

☐ US citizens contacted by a known KGB or other foreign agent operating under diplomatic immunity as an embassy official.

☐ American associates of a dissident who travels to a foreign country and knowingly or unknowingly meets espionage agents.

☐ Those in the United States connected with an organization that has shown up in a sinister fashion in CIA intelligence-gathering overseas.

Here, too, it must be noted that certain gray areas in the CIA charter may have served as a pretext for an agency anxious to preserve the national security against apparent threats:

"The Director of Central Intelligence shall be responsible for protecting intelligence sources and methods from unauthorized disclosure."

The agency is empowered "to perform for the benefit of the existing intelligence agencies such additional services of common concern as the National Security Council determines can be more efficiently accomplished centrally."

Sam Papich, an FBI agent who was liaison man with the CIA for eighteen years until his retirement in 1970, told the Washington *Post* the CIA statute ranged "from the vague to the ridiculous." He said CIA operations often blended into domestic areas for seemingly legitimate and certainly expedient reasons.

Papich routinely dealt with these domestic activities between the FBI and CIA. Often, he said, CIA experience in various foreign countries was of great value in assisting an FBI domestic investigation with foreign implications. In other cases, the handling of sensitive situations involving defectors called for both CIA and FBI agents.

Noting that each year about two thousand Americans are approached by Soviet espionage agents here and abroad, Papich gave a hypothetical example:

"If you get a report that Molly Brown while she was in Moscow was approached, what do you do? Nine times out of ten she's a good girl, but maybe naive, and nothing happened."

Papich said that nonetheless, the CIA might well open a file on "Molly Brown" even though she was back in this country since it was the CIA that originally uncovered her contact with a Soviet agent.

Personal Liberties vs. the Nation's Existence

Despite the continuing evidence of activities directed toward the destruction of the United States, the CIA controversy eloquently illustrates that many Americans seem more worried about some imagined infringement of their personal liberties than about very real threats to the nation's existence.

So far the CIA "spy" debate has been carried on under the assumption that somehow we have magically entered a new era of international tranquillity in which there are no longer "unfriendly nations." How strange it is that no other nation has entered this wonderful era and thus proceeded to tear down its anachronistic intelligence network.

Soviet agents now routinely "work" Capitol Hill and have used congressional staff people for their purposes. Under the guise of working out trade deals, other Soviet operatives work at a subtle and patient espionage. And there is disturbing evidence that American soil has become a battleground for the struggles of various foreign powers. In 1973, the year in which the CIA domestic operation apparently was halted, these news items aroused temporary if any interest among Americans:

March 6—Three rental cars, each packed with explosives, were found parked near three Israeli business establishments. A federal grand jury has indicted an Iraqi citizen, Khalid Al-Jawary, now a fugitive, for the crime.

April 16—In Washington, D.C., shots were fired into the bedroom window of a New Zealand diplomat's home. Police believe it was an attempt on the life of a Jordanian diplomat who had recently moved from the house. In red paint beneath the window was a call for "Death to the Zionists and their functionaries," signed "Black September."

July 1—Colonel Yosef Alon, an Israeli military attaché, was shot to death outside his suburban Washington home by what police believe was "an Arab commando team."

Incidents like these seem to pass quickly out of the memory of press and public caught up in concern that somebody may have been "spied upon." Seldom is an attempt made to evaluate the situation and determine whether or not that particular person might have well merited suspicion.

The CIA case is the crest of a wave of anti-intelligence mania that has swirled around the FBI, the Army, state and local police in recent years. It is not a random thing and it has been carefully orchestrated by the Left. One of the chief motivating forces has been the liberal Center for National Security Studies.

CNSS won some press attention last fall by calling a conference to discuss ways to do away with covert intelligence operations in the United States. Great emphasis was placed on using ultraliberal congressmen and sympathetic press people to attack intelligence gathering. Washington columnist Paul Scott cites Massachusetts Congressman [Michael] Harrington [Democrat] and Seymour Hersh as having "close ties with CNSS." . . .

It may well be that the CIA charter of 1947 should be more sharply defined, but this should be done with the realities of the dynamic fluidity of global espionage and sabotage operations clearly in mind. Where, indeed, does a "foreign operation" begin or end in these times?

It is certainly hoped that some semblance of sanity will overtake those so zealous about the congressional investigations. It will certainly not be useful to expose our vital intelligence-gathering machinery in an atmosphere of "circus" hearings. They should be closed hearings, carried out in an atmosphere of reason. We have already made it difficult for our allies' intelligence services to work with us for fear of sudden exposure and embarrassment.

IV. INDIVIDUAL PRIVACY CASES

EDITOR'S INTRODUCTION

Any comprehensive review of recent court cases or new legislation affecting individuals' privacy rights would be endless. This section touches on a few that have aroused considerable attention.

What, for example, are the dangers to privacy inherent in the widespread use of Social Security numbers? And what future use of the numbers is likely? This issue is dealt with by Dori Jones in the first article in this section. The confidentiality of credit card and banking systems records is next examined by Paul Armer of the Center for Advanced Study in the Behavioral Sciences. Jerrold Oppenheim, editor of *Cable Report*, then inquires into the possible misuse, so far as privacy is concerned, of the growing two-way cable TV systems.

Two privacy topics of recent concern are those relating to medical and student records. Natalie Davis Spingarn, a writer specializing in health care, writes of the "Eavesdroppers Behind the Doctor's Door." The recently enacted Family Educational Rights and Privacy Act of 1974, the so-called Buckley Act, is then examined in regard to rights to student records.

This section ends on a three-way approach to the right of privacy versus the rights of a free press. An overview of the problems involved is given by Martin Arnold, a New York *Times* analyst. Alan L. Otten, a Washington correspondent for the *Wall Street Journal*, asks how much we should or need to know about the President's health or that of presidential aspirants. Finally W. H. Hornby, vice president and executive director of the Denver *Post* and chairman of the Freedom of Information Committee of the American Society of Newspaper Editors, considers what balance is needed regarding secrecy, privacy, and publicity in the press.

SOCIAL SECURITY NUMBERS AND PRIVACY [1]

Everywhere you turn someone seems to be asking for your Social Security number—when you open a checking account, when you apply for a driver's license, when you buy a savings bond, often when you apply for a credit card or a job. More than your phone number, your license-plate number, or any of the other numbers you deal with every day—more even than your name, for many persons—the Social Security number has become the one identity that follows wherever you go.

Is the Social Security number on its way to becoming an all-purpose identifying number for Americans? Some say that result is inevitable; others are fighting against it as a potentially dangerous invasion of privacy.

In Sweden a similar system of personal identification seems to work. Each baby is assigned a number that follows it from cradle to grave, to be used for everything from a credit purchase at a store to tax and criminal records. The system has the advantages of transcending name changes caused by marriage or adoption, of efficiency for the record keepers, and of reduction of fraud caused by misidentification. And the Swedes also don't have to keep track of a different eight- or nine-digit number for every transaction.

But such a universal personal identifier can have serious consequences if no appropriate safeguards are instituted against misuse—particularly in the computer age—of personal information stored under it.

"It's not the number that's the evil, and it's not the information that's the evil; it's the decision to collect and use the information," says Hope Eastman, a lawyer for the

[1] From "Name Droppers," by Dori Jones, former staff writer. *National Observer*. p 8. S. 6, '75. Reprinted with permission from *The National Observer*, copyright Dow Jones & Company, Inc. 1975.

American Civil Liberties Union, which, she says, stands "unalterably opposed" to the expansion of the Social Security number to a universal identifier.

> The ultimate thing would be that citizens can be tracked by the government from cradle to grave. It wipes out the possibility of making a clean start [she continues]. It is also a mechanism of social control. The more information they have, the less creative, less adventurous, less politically active you are for fear of offending someone.

Expanding Use of Social Security Numbers

The expanding use of the Social Security number confuses many people because the innocuous-looking card itself reads, "For Social Security purposes—not for identification." This legend, however, means only that the card cannot be relied upon as positive evidence of the bearer's identity, not that information about the person cannot be stored in computers under that number.

The Social Security Board itself was the first to expand use of the number in 1937 when it authorized use of the number for state unemployment-insurance programs. The number became nearly universal in this country in 1961 when the Internal Revenue Service began demanding that taxpayers include it on tax records. Because of this decision, all individuals who earn money must furnish their numbers to their sources of income: employers, savings-and-loan institutions, corporations that pay dividends, insurance companies, and so forth. Children of wealthy parents must be given Social Security numbers as infants if trust funds are established in their names.

Likewise, because they need the Social Security numbers of their employees to report their earnings, many large companies use the number as an identifier in employee records. Some companies are now reversing this trend. IBM, for instance, has removed Social Security numbers from materials that are seen by employees and the public, such as company identification cards; the company has never used the number to identify employees in its records. The company also no longer asks prospective employees to supply their numbers on job applications. Both actions are a result of IBM's "respect for the individual's privacy," according to a company spokesman.

During the sixties, new uses for the number multiplied. The military began to use it as an ID number for servicemen. Schools were authorized to issue it to ninth graders "for both automatic data processing and control purposes." Many states began putting the numbers on driver's licenses, and banks were required to obtain them for each checking account.

Congress recently passed a law requiring applicants for aid to families with dependent children to supply not only their own numbers but that of each of their children. This stipulation is designed to check welfare fraud by ensuring that women do not "borrow" each other's children to get more benefits. The Social Security number has faults, however, that prevent it from being an effective standard universal identifier. According to *Records, Computers, and the Rights of Citizens,* a 1973 report by a special committee appointed by the Department of Health, Education, and Welfare (HEW), the Social Security number falls significantly short on several criteria for an ideal standard universal identifier.

Its most serious flaw is that it is easy for a person to obtain more than one number; more than 4.2 million Americans had two or more when the report was written. Sometimes numbers are mistakenly used by more than one person, such as the infamous 078-05-1120, which appeared on a sample card in a wallet advertisement; at one time more than five thousand wage earners used that number.

Also, the Social Security number is not entirely reliable because it does not have a check-digit to catch errors of transcription or oral reporting. The number does, however, nearly fit other criteria of permanence, ubiquity, availability, and indispensability.

Do We Need a Universal Identifier?

The important question is not so much whether the Social Security number makes a good universal identifier, but rather do we want or need such an identifier?

The answer is no, according to the HEW committee on automated personal-data systems, consisting of twenty-five persons with widely diverse viewpoints. The committee said in its 1973 report:

We recommend against the adoption of any nationwide, standard, personal identification format, with or without the SSN [Social Security number] that would enhance the likelihood of arbitrary or uncontrolled linkage of records about people. . . . What is needed is a halt to the drift toward an SUI [standard universal identifier] and prompt action to establish safeguards providing legal sanctions against abuses of automated personal-data systems.

The Privacy Act of 1974 followed through on some of the committee's suggestions, but did not eliminate the exchange of personal data. Within a governmental department, such as HEW, employees still have access to the data banks of other HEW agencies on a "need to know" basis.

"People don't link records because the number is there; the number is a convenient tool," says Carole Watts Parsons, who served as associate executive director to the HEW committee and was recently appointed executive director of the new Privacy Protection Study Commission.

The Privacy Act did, however, call a moratorium on the use of the Social Security number by federal agencies that did not have legal authority to require the number before this year. But this moratorium does not extend outside government.

However, a House bill introduced this year by Edward I. Koch, a New York City Democrat, and Barry M. Goldwater Jr., a California Republican, would prohibit private institutions from demanding that an individual disclose his or her Social Security number for a business transaction.

But so far the bill, numbered—appropriately, some think—
HR 1984, is for discussion purposes only, since no action is
likely to be taken on it until the effects of the Privacy Act
can be seen.

COMPUTERIZED BANKING [2]

On the front page of the New York *Times* . . . [in 1974]
there appeared the expression *nutritionally endangered*. Do
you know what they couldn't bring themselves to say? *Starving*.

Now, electronic funds transfer system (EFTS) is a high-
faluting way of describing a system that will replace money,
check and credit card transactions (some, not all, the proponents will hasten to add) with a system that will eventually be on-line from the point of sale to your bank's computer. And when you make a purchase the amount of the
sale will be debited to your account. (And thus the piece of
plastic you use is called a debit card rather than a credit
card.) Or you may elect to buy on credit, a distinction which
isn't relevant to the primary question, since in both instances the information about the sale reaches the computer
in real time and is recorded. (Experts guess that there are
now about 300 billion transactions in cash per year; about
75 percent for less than $1, and only 5 percent exceeding
$10.)

Checks are involved in a transaction only about a tenth
as often as cash; 90 percent are for greater than $10. And
1 percent are greater than $10,000 but account for 80 percent
of the dollar value. It costs roughly 20 cents to process a
check, making a rounded total cost of our demand deposit
accounting on the order of $10 billion. The number of
checks has been growing at about 7 percent per year.

[2] From "Keeping Your Bills Secret in an Electronic Age," by Paul Armer,
coordinator for the program on technology and society, Center for Advanced
Study in the Behavioral Sciences, Stanford, Calif. *Privacy Journal*. No. 5:1+. Mr.
'75. Copyright 1975 Robert Ellis Smith. Reprinted by permission.

Credit card transactions are about one fifth as frequent as check transactions; though, in recent years, they've been growing at about a 35 percent increase per year. Only 60 percent of the credit card transactions are for more than $10. There are about 35 million card holders in the United States. At an assumed average cost of 25 cents, the system cost is only about $100 million not including the cost of the credit verification systems.

In summary, cash transactions represent about 90 percent of the total, but, of the transactions over $10, only about one third are for cash.

There are two nationwide bank credit card systems—BankAmericard and Interbank Master Charge. Each has an electronic nationwide credit authorization system. National BankAmericard (NBI) has brought up a system to handle interbank transfers electronically. Thus, if you make a charge today with your BankAmericard and the merchant gets the chit to his bank today, later tonight that transaction will be in the records of your bank. And the cost is 2.5 cents. That means that country club billing (you get a copy of the receipt you signed in the store) is a thing of the past, although some banks will print facsimiles to try to keep you happy. Descriptive billing is what most of us will be forced to accept.

Both BankAmericard and Master Charge are busily designing systems that will connect, electronically, point-of-sale recorders in a store and remote bank teller machines to your bank's computer, debiting the sale amount to your account (or recording it for future debiting) all in real time. Implementation will begin . . . [in 1975].

There now exist four so-called automated clearinghouses which support the automatic deposit of payroll checks and automatic preauthorized payment of fixed monthly debts, like mortgage or car payments. Some of them also provide a service called "bill check." Here, for example, the local utility sends you a bill, part of which is a check which you sign and return to the utility. They batch the bill checks and transmit the data, not the checks, to the local automated clearinghouse, which debits your bank which then debits your account. This is not now on-line, but like the present systems of the bank credit card companies, could be upgraded.

This procedure is not now heavily used although Equitable Life Assurance Society, working with Chase Manhattan Bank, has its monthly transaction volume of preauthorized payments up to about 100,000. The thrift institutions are moving rapidly in implementing EFTS systems. MINTS (Mutual Institutions National Transfer Systems, Inc.) permits its card holders to do any banking business they might do at their home bank at any other MINTS member bank. MINTS' avowed hope is eventually to tie this service into a national network "hopefully managed by the Federal Reserve Board." One almost gets the impression that the commercial banks and the bank credit card systems are racing toward implementation of true real-time EFTS to get there before the thrift institutions and the Federal Reserve Board. Of course they're also much interested in the cost savings this will bring them.

What of the Federal Reserve System?

And what is the Federal Reserve System doing? For some time all checks in excess of $10,000 have been cleared electronically over "Fed wire." Remember that such checks are 1 percent of the total number but represent 80 percent of the dollar volume. Since 1947 the proportion of total deposits under the direct control of the Federal Reserve System has dropped from 86 to 77 percent and the pace of dropouts has been increasing. So the Federal Reserve System aspires, in my belief, to have "a" (and preferably "the") EFTS, which every bank would have to use. And, in order to use it, each bank would have to be a member of the Federal Reserve System. The Fed published a proposal to expand the Board's Regulation J, which governs the use of the Fed's facilities to collect checks, so as to permit the electronic transfer of funds (November 15, 1973). The Fed solicited comments on the proposed changes, but mentioned only economic and financial implications. In thirty-seven pages of material nothing was said about social implications —the word privacy does not appear. Little was said about security and access.

They received over two hundred responses. They've been silent ever since. They give the impression that they'd prefer it if we'd leave them alone and cease saying there may be social implications.

But while silent they haven't been inactive. The Fed, the Treasury and the Social Security Administration have begun depositing Social Security checks directly into the recipient's bank account in Georgia through the local automated clearinghouse. Florida recipients will be added in April and by 1976 the scheme will be implemented nationwide. The Treasury wants to cease entirely writing checks for routine periodic purposes.

The National Science Foundation has given a grant to Arthur D. Little, Inc. to do an assessment of "Less Cash/Less Check Technology." They published a first phase report in February 1974 and said on page 101: "In latter phases we will investigate how deep and how broad the concern for privacy is and how it will impede change in the payments system." . . .

That's like being concerned only over the public's opinion of whether smoking is dangerous to one's health and how that concern will impede the sale of cigarettes. Investigation of whether or not EFTS represents a threat to privacy seems not to be a question to be addressed!

One expert predicts that by 1980 one third of all purchases will utilize the bank debit-card system, replacing about 70 percent of check utilization in the process.

The important variables to me are whether the transaction from beginning until it reaches my bank is on-line or not and what percentage of the transactions, particularly those more than $10, are other than cash. The extreme case, in which all transactions go through the system in real time, obviously represents the greatest threat to privacy. It is unlikely that we'll get to the extreme case in the near future, if ever.

Several years ago I was a member of a team which was given the assignment of assuming that we were data processing advisers to the Russian Secret Police (the KGB) and then designing a system for maintaining surveillance of all Soviet citizens and foreigners within the USSR boundaries. After some study, we decided that the easiest and cheapest way to do it was to install a real-time EFTS which would handle all financial transactions. You see, such a system knows where an individual is in real time, as well as what he is buying, every time he makes a financial transaction. A system that knows where each individual is represents a great surveillance system for would-be tyrants. You can't alleviate my misgivings with legislation against using the system in that fashion since, in one of my scenarios, there has been a takeover of the government and all civil liberties suspended in the national interest. Legislation would be meaningless.

But much less extreme cases disturb me. In our existing payments systems, privacy is assured under all but the most unusual circumstances by the sheer cost and inconvenience of a manual search. EFTS, even non-real-time EFTS, would concentrate an enormous amount of financial information about an individual in one place—intimate details of his personal life.

CABLE TV AND PRIVACY [3]

Someday we may be shopping, banking, taking medical examinations and reading over cable television. Terminals will be installed in every living room, just as telephones and

[3] From "I Wonder Who's Watching Me Now," by Jerrold Oppenheim, editor of Cable Report. Cable Report. 4:1-2. Ja. '75. Copyright © 1974 by Assn. of Working Press, Inc. Reprinted by permission.

televisions are today. The cable will have two-way capability: while you are watching your TV set, your TV set may be keeping track of you.

The cable system manufacturers' boasts are ominous. "[I]t is essential that it be kept in mind that the TOCOM [cable TV] system . . . does have the capability of interrogating literally any information at remote points and transmitting this information back to a Central Data Terminal." As the advertising literature for this new system points out, its computer "is programmed to determine if the TV Receiver is on or off and what channel has been selected."

TOCOM has already been installed in several Texas communities. It can interrogate up to 180,000 home televisions in 30 seconds. If a burglar alarm were hooked up to the system and an interrogation electronically discovered an open window, the next step, according to the manufacturer, is that "based upon information received from the Remote Transmitter Receivers [two-way TV sets], we can automatically alert the police department."

That may sound like an efficient way to catch a burglar in the act. But the same technology can be easily exploited for less socially useful purposes. "[S]ince we can determine who is turned to what channel . . . If customer 741 in Group One turns on his switch and turns to Channel 13 . . . at 10:30 in the morning then we will know within thirty seconds of when he turns his set on . . . and likewise we will know within thirty seconds of when he changed to a different channel." "For the future of the system, with very little modification," the same manufacturer says, "we see the capability of . . . the control of devices at remote locations . . . we may in one condition disable every remote home transmitter receiver throughout the system; . . . or we can, by transmitting an identification code, along with a separate code, selectively enable or disable each respective remote transmitter unit."

In other words, your TV set can be turned on in the middle of the night from outside your home. Likewise, someone who knows to which channel you are tuned can turn your set off.

The president of K'Son Corporation, an electronics firm in Fullerton, California, recently wrote about a similar piece of equipment of which he is very proud. "It automatically responds to [electronic] interrogations from the head-end with information on what channel is being watched and when. Also it has the built-in capability of being turned on and off from the head-end by the transmission of a unique code."

These systems were primarily for the apparently harmless purpose of simplifying pay-cable billing. But less innocuous uses for the technology are easily found. Tokyo's Takanaw Prince Hotel uses its cable TV system to monitor the missing contents of room refrigerators, thus simplifying its billing procedures. Ex-President Nixon once suggested a civil defense warning system that would have automatically turned on every radio and television set in the nation and tuned them all to the same emergency message. He never explained what might constitute an "emergency."

Viewers of the experimental Rediffusion cable system in Dennisport, Massachusetts, select programs by dialing an instrument similar to a telephone. Each dial moves a mechanical switch in the central office and anyone sitting in that office can see exactly to which channel every set is tuned and whether or not each set is on. There is not even a safeguard against a person in the central office moving the mechanical switches until each set is tuned to the channel he has chosen.

Cable television may become the method of distribution for library books, newspapers, and news magazines within twenty years. One of the simplest things for a cable system to record will be the names of books and periodicals each household has requested. Similarly, a system could monitor political speeches watched. The danger of this ability was well explained by recently retired Senator Sam J. Ervin (Democrat, North Carolina) in a similar context. "When people fear surveillance, *whether it exists or not,* when they grow afraid to speak their minds and hearts freely to their government or to anyone else, then we shall cease to be a free society."

With two-way cable TV so close on the horizon, it is alarming that so little attention has been paid to the privacy issue. The Federal Communications Commission (FCC) has not seriously grappled with the problems of privacy on cable TV, although it has received information on the subject.

What Technological Protections?

Yet there are some reasonably simple technological protections available. For example, Donald Chandler, executive vice president of Electronic Industrial Engineering, Inc., had not thought about the problem before he testified to the Illinois commission. But, under questioning, he estimated that one fourth of a system could be effectively set aside and made relatively private for an increase in construction cost for the entire system of about 7 percent—an addition of perhaps 70 cents to a $10 monthly charge. The technology for this is reasonably simple. Systems that scramble and unscramble pictures (used also for pay-TV) cost about $25 per unit to manufacture. For even less, a cable operator can install a light and bell to notify a subscriber when his television is being monitored to determine which channel is being tuned. A switch to prevent such monitoring is also inexpensive.

In fact, according to the Electronic Industries Association (the electronic manufacturers' trade group), a cable "network . . . can enjoy *any* desired degree of privacy *that can be economically justified.*"

However, what a clever engineer can devise to protect privacy on the cable, an equally clever engineer can undo. Thus, at best, you are guaranteed of being monitored (surveyed as to channel watched, cassette requested, etc.) and tapped (directly overheard) only by professionals.

If a portion of the cable spectrum were reserved by law for private communications, then scrambling devices of relatively high sophistication could be installed on those channels at special studios. In addition, locks and armored cable should be installed to deter access to terminal boards and cable drops from pole to house and within a house. Anyone who has prowled around in an apartment house basement knows how easy it is to tap into a naked telephone line strung along beams in the cellar below.

Technological solutions of this character are feasible if they are built into the system when it is constructed, but they are worthwhile only if methods for circumventing them are not built into the system or added later. Legislation is clearly in order, since there is little incentive for the operator either to include such solutions in the cable system or to prevent their circumvention.

While legally required technological protections will discourage monitoring and tapping, they should be supplemented with purely legal protections. For one thing, disclosure of information obtained via cable could be forbidden or allowed only after notice and opportunity to refuse consent. No disclosure would be permissible except with express consent (which might even be bought, as, for example, by audience rating services). Consent should be required at each occasion (simply a matter of pushing a button on a two-way cable set) and in either case should not be made a condition of subscribing to a cable service. Minimum mandatory penalties should be high and enforceable by the district attorney, the FCC, and the injured individual. A new right of legal action ought to be specifically established for invasion of privacy by unauthorized monitoring or tapping of a cable.

An obvious problem in enforcing such a right is detecting when information is being obtained from the cable. In the case of monitoring, detection is relatively simple since an interrogating signal must normally be sent to the set.

Taps of the cable, on the other hand, are extremely difficult to detect, since tapping merely deflects a minute proportion of the transmitted signal. Only very expensive, sophisticated equipment can detect the presence of a tap. Tapping can therefore only be eliminated by rigorous policing, a function that can be most efficiently performed by the system operator. The operator of any cable system must maintain the physical security of the cable to insure adequate service to subscribers; he therefore can already provide coarse physical surveillance against taps. Besides, in order to prevent pirating of service, some operators have installed sophisticated electronic gear to detect signal losses due to unauthorized connection of additional sets to a cable terminal. It would not be difficult to attune such equipment to detecting taps that invade the privacy of subscribers.

To encourage operators to do this policing, it might be appropriate to reward them for each tap detected. To increase the incentive, the operator could be strictly liable to all persons whose communications are illegally monitored or tapped. High mandatory punitive damages could be included.

Since most of tomorrow's cable systems are not yet built, especially in the largest cities, it is relatively easy now to build in such protections of privacy as scramblers and warning signals. It is also possible to add these safeguards later—just as it is theoretically possible to add similar protection now to the telephone system—but it is much more expensive in both technological and political costs.

PRIVACY AND MEDICAL PRACTICE [4]

Whatsoever I shall see or hear in the course of my profession in my intercourse with men, if it be what should not be noised abroad, I will never divulge, holding such things to be holy secrets.—*Oath of Hippocrates*

[4] From "Eavesdroppers Behind the Doctor's Door," by Natalie Davis Spingarn, a freelance writer specializing in health care. Washington *Post.* p C 1-2. Je. 1, '75. © The Washington Post. Reprinted by permission.

Hippocrates, hear these tales of the 1970s:

☐ A surgeon, hospitalized for a mild heart attack, returns home to find his auto liability insurance has been canceled. He phones his broker, discovers that he has mysteriously been found to be less of an "approved risk" than he was before. No one has tried to examine him to see if there has been any change in his capability as a driver. Evidently, his health and auto insurance companies had traded information.

☐ A talented young woman hunts a job after her college graduation. After many painful rejections, she discovers that potential employers are put off by an entry in her university file made by her sixth grade teacher: "Melinda's mother is emotionally unstable." The teacher, neither a psychiatrist nor a psychologist, had met the mother only casually, yet the entry followed Melinda for years without anyone's questioning its propriety, reliability or relevance.

☐ A file clerk is being considered for a promotion. She does not get the job and hears from her fellow workers it is because she has been seeing a psychiatrist (they heard it from friends in the personnel office who process insurance forms). When she asks the boss if this is true, he says it is—and reports her psychiatrist has diagnosed her as schizophrenic.

☐ Credit bureau investigators visit the neighbors of an accountant who has had a cancer operation and has filed a claim to cover his hospitalization and surgery costs. They want to know if the neighbors feel the operation has affected the accountant's work potential.

No doubt about it, Hippocrates' "holy secrets," traditionally guarded by doctor and patient, are now often noised about and with some peculiar results. The medical examination room is getting crowded. You think you are talking to your doctor, but insurance companies, lawyers, future educators or employers, researchers—even credit bureaus—may be listening in.

There are doctors who would risk going to jail rather than reveal their patients' secrets, even to the courts. But some doctors gossip—they say such and such a patient cannot handle money or was married too many times; they take their telephone calls in front of family and friends; they entertain at parties with juicy case histories, only loosely masked. If either curious spouse or hungry lawyer stand among the listeners, the results may be disastrous.

A New York psychiatrist recently wrote a book about the seven-year treatment of an unnamed patient, her husband and their son. The patient sought to enjoin distribution of the book as an invasion of privacy. Indeed, it did reveal the most intimate details of the lives, secret thoughts and fantasies of the patient and her family. (The masking was so loose that they could be easily recognized by the most casual acquaintance—the patient was also a psychotherapist, the musically gifted son had written three operas, and so forth. Hardly a family to be lost in a crowd.) The author contended the book was of significant scientific merit. The "agonized decision" of the mental health professional organizations has been to support the patient. Recently the Supreme Court refused to review the case before trial, with the result that the book will not be distributed pending trial in the lower courts.

Why the Erosion in Confidentiality?

How did it happen? How has this extraordinary departure from the letter and spirit of the Hippocratic Oath come about? Why has a gradual erosion in physician-patient confidentiality occurred throughout our society?

Not too many years back, medical record-keeping was a comparatively simple business, like much else of the business of living.

The family doctor knew his patients, often long and well. He filed facts about their health in the safe crevices of his mind or on 3x5 cards—from birth through childhood

sickness and accidents to chronic disease and terminal illness.

Now there are more, and more different kinds, of us—
patients and practitioners alike. We move more, travel more
and take advantage of the training and skills of more spe-
cialists. Our doctors and their numerous assistants must
record and file our health histories so they can communicate
with each other, and treat successfully.

Our doctors must know. The problem is that others
must know, too—sometimes. Those responsible for conta-
gious-disease control must know when an epidemic of small-
pox or measles breaks out. Criminal-justice officials must be
able to check a mental patient's history. Carriers must assure their customers that aircraft pilots or bus operators are
in top condition. Insurers must verify claims to prevent
abuse and spiraling premium costs. Medical researchers
can unravel nature's secrets only by studying individual
histories. (A recent example: two-generation research which
established the connection between stilbesterol treatment of
pregnant women and clear-cell vaginal cancer in their
daughters years later.)

Technological and "Third Party" Involvement

Two powerful trends, one technological and one social,
have made it easy for health records—once secure in the
privacy of the doctor's office or hospital records-room and
available only to medical personnel—to be abstracted again
and again and forwarded, often without "consent," to the
invisible and unknown inquirers.

One is the great surge in computer technology, and with
it, the increased feeding of personal health information into
machines which can handle many millions of instructions a
second and store vast quantities of material.

There are, as Harvard Professor Arthur R. Miller has
noted, dangers here: As information accumulates, the contents of the individual dossier tend to appear more and
more impressive despite the dubious accuracy of the data.

The fat file bespeaks reliability, as does the myth of computer infallibility. And the centralization of information
from widely divergent sources creates serious risks of using
facts out of context. Whose business is it, after all, that a
patient once consulted an internist about impotence or a
heart condition?

The other main trend which tends to increase access to
our health records is the growth of "third party" involvement in health matters. With the majority of Americans
covered to some extent by health—or at least by hospital—
insurance, more and more people not responsible for our
health care are asking questions about it—and processing the
answers. Americans visit the doctor 1.3 billion times a year
and complete at least 28 million hospital stays. Most of us
do not contemplate, indeed do not know, that those receiving the records of visits to doctor and hospital may feed
them, warts and all, into the memories of their computers
and, through network arrangements, into those of a growing number of data centers throughout the country.

The Medical Information Bureau (MIB) for instance, a
computerized center for medical data set up by the insurance industry, is available to hundreds of commercial companies. The Multistate Information System (MIS), containing complete mental health histories, links psychiatric hospitals, clinics and outpatient health centers in the New
England area.

In the public sector, Medicare, Medicaid and other public health programmers already are keeping millions of
health records. Now the new PSROs (Peer Standards Review Organizations) will add their demands to those of
government insurers and cost justifiers. They will need vast
amounts of personal information to profile practitioners and
in other ways to see to it that medical services rendered by
the Medicare, Medicaid and maternal and child health programs are necessary and of high quality.

A discomforting specter has turned up to haunt us, nine
years short of 1984: We are all hooked up to the Big Com-

puter. Facts about your heart condition, my ulcer, the neigh-
boring child's mental retardation, recorded when we visit
doctors and clinics or stay in the hospital, are transferred
automatically in to the data system of a national health insurance program tied to the computers of other social benefit programs—perhaps even to those of the Internal Revenue Service. No overall, enforceable confidentiality rules or
guidelines control the system—who feeds what information,
who has access to that information and for what purposes.
Our health secrets are instantly retrievable, in this country
and in others, for the rest of our lives and beyond. Tap into
the system in Oregon, find out about the heartbeat, the
cancer, the psychological dreams and fantasies of the patient in the District of Columbia.

That is the specter.

The Medical Establishment Faces Up

Oddly enough, the event that caused the medical establishment finally to face up to the specter had nothing to do
with computers which, after all, work according to human
demand and reflect a man-made culture. It was the snoops
who broke into psychiatrist Dr. Lewis Fielding's California
office looking for Daniel Ellsberg's records who shook the
elders from their lethargy. The Nixon political operatives
testifying before the Senate Watergate Committee finished
the job. They did not seem to realize they had done anything wrong. "You mean to say, Mr. Ehrlichman, that you
don't know psychiatrists are physicians?" asked Senator Sam
Ervin, eyeing the witness sternly under the television klieg
lights.

Evidently not. Stung by such a cavalier attitude, and
fearful of the extent to which it might reflect a general erosion in physician-patient confidentiality, the American Psychiatric Association, representing some 22,000 practicing
psychiatrists, began a series of meetings with a wide range of
other medical, legal and consumer groups. These culminated last fall [1974] in a Confidentiality Conference held,

ironically, at Key Biscayne, Florida. Some fifty organizations sent representatives. They ranged from the American Medical Association and American College of Surgeons to the National Congress of Parents and Teachers, the Mental Health Law Project and the American Civil Liberties Union.

The Key Biscayne conference did not attempt fully to answer the complex questions raised at its meetings. Rather, its sessions outlined the magnitude of the problems and the chief areas of concern and voted to establish a commission to address them in depth.

Plans call for the commission to get under way . . . [in 1975]. Some may feel its job will be an easy one: just curb requests for health information, tell doctors and hospitals to stop giving out medical facts indiscriminately to nonmedical snoops.

Records vs. Confidentiality

But exquisitely delicate balances must be struck between the patient's right to privacy and the society's need to know. These include:

☐ The balance between the minimum required to keep meaningful records and the maximum needed to protect confidentiality.

How to define the health record? How to ascertain what should go in, what should remain, what should stay out? How to determine to what extent the scrivener's hand should be stayed, in view of the risks involved, so that some information at least is lost to society's memory or retained only in a limited way?

It stands to reason you do not have to worry about what does not go into the record in the first place. Obviously, some information is needed to write an adequate medical record. Equally obviously, other information—anecdotal gossip, for example—is not.

In between lies a gray area—information which might

or might not be needed for the sake of the patient's health, now or in the future. Take children's records. Doctors are usually trained to track a child's health over the years, collecting "longitudinal data" with an eye to preventing future illnesses. This practice usually generates extensive records full of tentative judgments and guesswork—social, environmental and biological. Such data about the health of a two-year-old could stay in his record seventy years!

Does all of it need to be there? Doubting it, some children's advocates hold that children's medical records—especially those of the deprived children who frequent courts and social welfare agencies—are often abused. Parole officers, welfare and other officials can frequently get hold of them at the spin of a telephone dial; they travel, unprotected, from agency to agency and many see them along the way, all in the name of "the best interests of the child."

The job of defining the health record is hard enough when you are dealing with files kept by doctors or hospitals for independent adults voluntarily seeking treatment; it is still harder when you consider records for children or dependent people of all ages kept by schools, colleges, prisons or military organizations. For such institutions, voluntary and involuntary, health care is of only secondary interests.

Some have suggested dual record keeping as a possible solution: the same doctor, the same patient, but different sets of records for different uses. This mind-boggling and perhaps impractical suggestion takes various forms, but all involve some sort of divorce between material which is confidential and that which is not—one antiseptic enough to be abstracted for third-party payers, researchers, judicial bodies and all the rest, the other for the doctor and his colleagues.

Cop-out? Critics say so, arguing that, especially in psychiatry, they need adequate, abstractable records to justify diagnosis and treatment. If the revealing little ways in which people deal with each other go into some sort of secondary "eyes only" record, doctors and hospitals may be left out on a limb. (A mental hospital which neglects officially to record why a patient was permitted to go out for the day, for instance, might wish it had done so when he is killed in an auto accident and the hospital is sued for damages.) And outsiders may find a way to get confidential notes anyway.

What's more, in a time when more and more medical personnel are involved in treatment, more communication is needed, not less. The words "seen by psychotherapist, July 11," or "acute cholecystitis-cholecystectomy 1974" no longer suffice when a whole team of professionals and paraprofessionals must follow complex instructions. Dual record keeping might result in all sorts of foul-ups.

Destroying Records vs. Research Needs

□ The balance between destroying health records or expunging them for the sake of personal privacy and keeping them for research contributing to science and to history.

What should stay in the health record? Should information be allowed to petrify, unchallenged, over the years? If it is not reexamined periodically, or its archaic nature brought to the attention of file users, warn the civil libertarians, there are human dangers. They cite cases like that of a schoolboy, sick with an infection, who fainted in class and was treated in the infirmary. Returning later, he glimpsed the note "Epilepsy?" in his medical file. Too terrified to discuss the matter, he carried with him for years the notion that he is an epileptic.

A number of worried physicians and patients would be ready to experiment with a new formula. Dual records would be kept for children—the doctor's working notes, containing hunches and unconfirmed diagnoses, and a permanent record belonging to the child-consumer and kept by him. The working record would be reviewed each time the patient saw the doctor; ultimately each piece of information would be either expunged or inserted into the permanent record. School health records, subject to more squirreling than almost any others, would be sealed for a period after graduation, and then destroyed.

On the other side of this particular confidentiality see-saw sit the medical historians, their eyes on a future when facts not now considered meaningful may become all-important. Boston University Medical School's Dr. Otto Marx, an historian and court psychiatrist, argues that too many records have already been lost.

As a result, Dr. Marx says, epidemiological research and genetic studies are difficult or impossible to carry out and we know practically nothing about the past incidence of mental illness. He urges that wherever possible we save records, while preserving confidentiality in tight compartments, to enable medicine to move into the next technological era without the loss of vital material.

Most people, Dr. Marx adds, have little concern about the publicity they may spark after their deaths. But—tip the seesaw back again—their families may be disturbed.

. . . [The daughter of] novelist F. Scott Fitzgerald and his wife Zelda was so upset by the psychiatric material in a biography of her mother that she could not finish reading the *Zelda* manuscript. The book documented her late mother's illness with reports on her stay at several well-known mental hospitals and clinics here and abroad. Who could have imagined that a person's intimate dreams and feelings, blurted out in moments of extreme stress to reputable doctors at outstanding institutions as part of one-to-one therapy, would be revealed to a researcher by these same doctors and institutions some forty years later?

Public Good vs. Personal Privacy

☐ The balance between sharing health records for the public good and limiting access for the sake of personal privacy.

Who can see health records? For what purpose? How much of a health record should be shown to an outsider and how much kept confidential? The professionals in medical recording are the first to say they need some sort of across-the-board regulations to help answer such questions.

All too often, they report, just put on a white coat and you have it made. There is a genial looseness about many hospital and clinic record-rooms, which results in file drawers left open or file folders scattered on empty desks during lunch breaks. Security experts counter that they can design "hardware" and "software" to make any personalized data system 95 percent secure. They can, they say, limit such a system to a small group of people whose access is authorized only after careful examination of their right to know—keeping "protector" files which record the identity of inquirers, coding sensitive material including vulnerable psychiatric material, even requiring finger or voice prints to get into secure areas. But such things are very expensive.

It is a matter of matching the security to the need. Someone is going to have to make some hard value-judgments as to what is needed—and if the medical professions and other such groups do not make them, the government will probably step in to do it for them.

Congress has already shown its concern with health records confidentiality. The peer review legislation mandates the development of coding procedures which will "provide maximum confidentiality as to patient identity." And it has teeth: a $1,000 fine and/or six months' imprisonment for inappropriate disclosure of information. The Department of Health, Education, and Welfare's strong draft confidentiality policy regulations . . . could have a ripple effect. It is significant that each of the major National Health Insurance proposals includes some form of peer review.

Sharing Medical Information

The most intriguing solutions proposed for health confidentiality problems center around the doctrine of "informed consent." This doctrine, once simply the patient's consent to a medical procedure, has come to mean also his consent to sharing that medical information with others. And this has come to include his right to see his own record to assure its accuracy and protect himself against mislabeling and misdiagnosis.

Think back on the last time you signed a health insurance claim form. Unless you are an extraordinary consumer —a veritable Ralph Nader—your consent was anything but "informed." It was probably given in a routine matter; you did not consider the possible consequences of words like these (most often in tiny type in an unobtrusive place on the page): "I hereby authorize the undersigned physician to release any information acquired in the course of my examination or treatment." Or, worse still, "To all physicians, hospitals, clinics, dispensaries, sanitariums, pharmacists, prepayment organizations, employers, unions and insurance companies: You are authorized to permit insurance company X or its representatives to obtain a copy of your records pertaining to the examination, treatment, history, prescriptions and benefit payments. . . ."

Many argue that the breadth of the "blanket" consent form in common use today makes it hard for doctors and institutions to deny information to third . . . [parties]—has not the patient given them permission to tell all? Narrowing the form so that patients can consent only to the disclosure of certain pertinent parts of their records is a needed reform. So is coding to mask especially sensitive diagnoses and conditions. Insurers and doctors could then refer to "Number 7", for example, instead of to the lurid symptoms of a psychiatric illness.

Benjamin Lipson, an executive with a Boston Life insurance company, reports the results of a survey which confirm a general suspicion: In the vulnerable field of psychiatry, some doctors do not answer insurance company requests for patient information fully and promptly, and many who do are very careful as to what facts they supply and in what

terms they supply them. (An Illinois psychiatrist even admitted distorting diagnosis for insurance purposes.)

The reasons for such medical evasiveness show up clearly
in the Lipson survey. More than three quarters of the nearly
nine hundred psychiatrists surveyed fear a breach of confidentiality in responding to insurance companies; half are
certain the companies do not preserve confidentiality. Although they feel, ironically, that patients under psychiatric
care are sometimes better risks than those who are not, almost all the respondents also tend to feel that psychiatric
information in the wrong hands might prejudice these same
patients' jobs.

Such fears are compounded in the complex legal area,
where psychiatrists must often make difficult decisions about
the disclosure of confidences—with and without patient consent. The American Psychiatric Association has officially
stated that its members have the "right to dissent within
the framework of the law," and Dr. Maurice Grossman, the
APA's expert on third-party confidentiality matters, has advised them not to be intimidated by legal subpoenas. Some
lawyers here advocate an approach used in Sweden, where a
psychiatrist treating a patient is not called upon to evaluate
or testify in court about the case. Instead another professional carries out these tasks.

Seeing One's Own Health Records

The newest aspect of the "informed consent" question
involves the concept of permitting a patient to see his own
health record so he can check its accuracy and correct errors.
(This principle is now embodied for other fields in federal
legislation such as the 1974 Privacy Act and the Buckley
amendment on school records, though the latter has caused
considerable difficulties for teachers and administrators.)
[See "Fruitful Privacy Efforts of Congress," in Section V,
below, and "Student Privacy Rights," in this section, below.] Many doctors fear the principle, most patients are
unaware of the issue, but the idea is gaining ground. Should

such a right be absolute or qualified? Should any patient be able to see his record, whether he is in a mental hospital or a surgical bed, whether or not a doctor judges him incompetent or simply unready to deal with the full details of an illness?

Such questions create polarization. At one end of the spectrum, a civil libertarian contends that "informed consent" would be meaningless if the patient did not have the right to see his record and that any doctor who attempts to deny that right should be compelled to obtain a court order supporting that decision. At the other, a psychiatrist who runs a private hospital says that, if he cannot be trusted to judge his patients' competence to deal with their records, he will go out of business.

Between the two poles are many who would limit the patient's right to see his record in some way. They would defer to the doctor's judgment in certain cases—when, for example, a patient is suffering from terminal cancer and cannot accept the truth. Or they would refer a doctor-patient disagreement to a second physician of the patient's own choosing or to some other "independent" judge.

Baffling problems remain. How can society strictly limit access to health records and, at the same time, firmly establish the patient's right to review them? How can names and other "identifiers" be stripped from records, thereby ensuring both privacy and the future research value of the medical information—and then reinserted so patients and their lawyers can review and challenge the record? Will both patient and doctor become so involved with the "informed consent" question that medical record-keeping changes for the worse—fit for patients' eyes perhaps but so bland as to be of little value to medical professionals?

Sometimes apathy triumphs over the right to know. One mental hospital recently offered patients the chance to see their records—and very few took advantage of the opportunity.

But it is clear that, whatever individual patients may do,

our computerized society hungers for personal information and that the varied demands for medical records will continue to grow. The issue can be met only by the development of clear rules balancing the needs of patient, practitioner, research, commerce and society itself. The task is complex, even infuriating, but not impossible of solution.

STUDENT PRIVACY RIGHTS[5]

The Health, Education, and Welfare Department Report entitled *Records, Computers, and the Rights of Citizens* (1973) defines the relationship between personal privacy and record keeping in the following way:

An individual's personal privacy is directly affected by the kind of disclosure and use made of identifiable information about him in a record. A record containing information about an individual in identifiable form must, therefore, be governed by procedures that afford an individual a right to participate in deciding what the content of the record will be, and what disclosure and use will be made of the identifiable information in it.

This winter [1974–1975], under new legislation known as the Buckley Act, students and their parents will be able to take the first steps toward a meaningful participation in deciding what kinds of information shall be held in their school records and how it shall be used.

The Family Educational Rights and Privacy Act, styled the Buckley Act after its leading sponsor, Senator James Buckley of New York, was passed in August 1974, then amended in the last hours of the 93d Congress. President Ford signed the amended act into law on New Year's Eve.

The initial intent of the act was simple, rational, and, in those preoccupied days last August, apparently noncontroversial. Students and their parents would be able to examine the contents of their school records, contest the

[5] From "Student Records: Your Rights Under the Buckley Act," by Trudy R. Hayden. *Privacy Report*. 2:1-9. F. '75. Reprinted by permission. *Privacy Report* is issued by The Project on Privacy and Data Collection/American Civil Liberties Union Foundation.

accuracy or propriety of certain entries, and exercise some control over the dissemination of information from the files. In our present topsy-turvy world, students usually cannot find out what is in their files, but almost anyone else can—teachers, administrators, social workers, health agencies, prospective employers, admissions officers of colleges and graduate schools, private testing services, to say nothing of police, probation officers, courts, the FBI. The Buckley Act was designed to turn matters right-side-up again.

The idea was neither radical nor novel: a dozen states and numerous local communities already had laws or regulations giving parents access to their children's files. Enforcement may have been somewhat lax, but the principle had been accepted and appeared to be gaining.

The legislation passed last August was introduced on the floor as an amendment to the General Education Provisions Act. No committee hearings had been held. Although the law clearly applied to institutions of higher learning, it was debated in Congress in the context of other legislation primarily concerned with elementary and secondary education. The new law apparently escaped the notice of the nation's colleges and universities at the time. Only as November 19, the effective date of the act, drew near did they take alarm at the impact the law might have upon their own record-keeping practices, traditionally committed to "confidentiality"—from, not for, their students.

Lobbyists for the colleges besieged Congress with demands for the act's amendment, pleading for exemptions, threatening to destroy their files, deriding the law as "unreasonable" and "unenforceable," and raising the specters of wholesale evasion, mass student demands for hearings on the "accuracy" of their marks, invasions of privacy through revelation of personal notes kept by teachers and counselors and financial statements submitted by parents, and the virtual collapse of the college admissions process.

The Senate was amenable to compromise and accepted a series of amendments in December. It was primarily through the dogged resistance of Representative John Brademas of Indiana, one of the House conferees, that the most damaging of the amendments were modified or dropped altogether. Many of the amendments that did pass merely clarified the intent of the original act; a few, however, significantly restricted its application.

On January 6 the Department of Health, Education, and Welfare published its proposed regulations for implementation of the act . . . [January 6, 1975].

Who Is Covered?

The Buckley Act applies to any "educational agency or institution" which receives federal funds administered through the Office of Education. This would encompass all public institutions and some private ones as well. Where students receive certain benefits directly (such as federal loans) but the institution itself receives none, the act will not apply.

The rights accorded by the act apply to *present and former* students. For elementary and secondary students under eighteen, these rights are exercised by the parents. Postsecondary students, and other students upon reaching the age of eighteen, termed *eligible students*, exercise their rights directly.

A great disappointment to ALCU (the American Civil Liberties Union) was the failure to extend coverage to rejected applicants to a school. Without the right to inspect the records and letters of recommendation submitted with their applications, unsuccessful applicants may never know why they didn't make it. This is not simply a matter of satisfying idle curiosity, as the following incidents show:

A law school dean received a letter from a professor at another law school about a student who wanted to transfer. The letter said that the student was dishonest and had cheated. The dean wrote the student, telling him the transfer application would be rejected, and why. In response, he received a letter from the other law school saying that the cheating accusation had been investigated and found to be unsubstantiated, and further, that the professor who made the accusation had not been invited to return to the faculty.

Another student was informed of his rejection for a graduate fellowship because a letter from a fellow student accused him of attempted homosexual rape. No one had ever investigated to determine if the charge was true.

In both cases, had the students not been informed of the reasons for their rejection, they would have been completely helpless to clear their records of serious charges that may have followed them for life. These incidents were unusual in that faculty members took the initiative to explain the basis for their decisions. In the ordinary course of events, rejected applicants are left in the dark. Their omission from the protections of the Buckley Act is a serious weakness in the law.

The proposed HEW regulations state that institutions may, under state or local laws or their own administrative practices, give students rights similar to parental rights under the act. The Buckley Act merely sets minimum standards. In fact, many states and local school boards have gone further, some allowing even the youngest grade school children to see their own files.

What Records Are Covered?

The act gives rights of access to "education records," defined as "those records, files, documents, and other materials which—(1) contain information directly related to a student; and (2) are maintained by an educational agency or institution, or by a person acting for such agency or institution."

Not included are the following:

1. Private notes maintained by instructors and school personnel solely as "memory aids" (such as a teacher's daily record book or notes jotted down by a counselor after a conference with a student), so long as they are not given or revealed to any other person except a substitute. Such notes

are not exempt if they are placed in a student's permanent file.

2. Records kept by a law enforcement unit such as a university security force, but only if these records are kept separate from the student's other records, are used solely for law enforcement purposes, and are not made available to anyone other than law enforcement officials of the same jurisdiction, and also only if these officials do not have access to the student's education records

3. Records kept on employees of the institution who are not enrolled students, if these relate solely to their role as employees and are not used for any other purpose

4. Records on postsecondary students eighteen or older which are used in connection with medical or psychiatric treatment and are available only to professionals or para-professionals engaged in their treatment. Students may request that these records be released to a physician of their own choice.

Further, the following records are not available for inspection by postsecondary students:

1. Their parents' financial records, such as copies of tax returns

2. Confidential letters of recommendation placed in the records prior to 1 January 1975, but only if these are used solely for the purposes originally intended. If a confidential letter written by a high school teacher as part of a student's college application in 1971 is passed on to a potential employer in 1975, the student may see that letter.

3. Letters of recommendation with respect to which students have waived their right of access. (See discussion under heading *Waivers* below.)

The matter of confidential letters of recommendation was easily the hottest issue in the December debate. Such letters have traditionally been written in confidence—though increasing numbers of teachers are adopting the practice of giving copies to their students. Spokesmen for the universities objected that without the protection of confidentiality, teachers will not be frank, but will write only bland, uninformative statements useless to admissions officers, and therefore undue reliance will be placed on grades and test scores in deciding on applicants.

Yet letters of so-called recommendation are particularly important to students because they contain precisely that kind of information which can be of greatest harm to them: subjective impressions, unverified accusations, judgments based on personal bias, even calculated malice. The revelation of such statements might be extremely embarrassing to the writer, but the student stands to lose a college education or a job, surely a greater risk.

Moreover, the contention that only secret references can be frank is patently untrue. If frankness is a virtue, why not frankness with students as well? Why couldn't a teacher simply say to a student, "I can give you a good recommendation on some counts, but I will also have to mention your weak points," and explain what these are? Then the student could decide either to ask for the letter anyway or try someone else. No embarrassment—and no nasty surprises months or years later. If letters of recommendation are as important to the decision-makers as the universities claim they are, it is all the more imperative that students know what is in them.

Congress compromised by exempting letters filed before January 1. So, those who have already suffered the adverse consequences of letters written in the past won't find much comfort in the Buckley Act. Some institutions tried to keep faith with both letter writers and students by destroying or returning to their writers letters filed before January 1. But many of these letters had already been copied and widely disseminated. Now there is no way for students to trace the letters or to know what kind of comments about themselves have made the rounds.

Waivers

Students may waive their right of access to confidential recommendations written after 1 January 1975 with respect to admission to an educational institution, application for employment, or receipt of an honor. Waivers must be in writing, and students must be notified, at their request, of the names of all persons submitting such confidential statements, including persons who send in unsolicited letters. These statements may be used only for their originally intended purpose (college admission, employment, or receipt of an honor, whichever category is designated in the waiver). Under no circumstances may an institution require a waiver as a condition of admission, receipt of financial aid, or other benefits and services.

This provision is the outcome of another compromise on the letter of recommendation question. ACLU opposed it. The Union argued that no waiver provision should be written into the law because a person is always free, without statutory authority, to waive a right or benefit. If a student wants a letter from a teacher who refuses to write unless confidentiality is promised, he or she could agree to that condition without statutory authorization. By including a waiver provision in the law, Congress might encourage institutions to extract waivers from their students.

It is true that the statute forbids the requirement of a waiver as a condition of admission, benefits, or services. But there is still scope for more subtle forms of coercion, by practice or "understanding" rather than any explicit rule. The waiver amendment could prove to be a dangerous loophole; its implementation will bear close watching.

Access

The proposed HEW regulations require institutions to notify parents and eligible students, at least annually and in their own language, of the following information:

1. what types of records directly related to the student are maintained

2. the names of persons responsible for the files

3. who may see the records without parental or student consent, and for what purposes

4. the institution's procedures for student and parental access to the records, for expungement of information, for hearings on contested information, and for copying records.

The institution must also notify students and parents of the categories of data that will be treated as "directory information." Under the act, directory information may be published and released to outsiders without parental or student consent. It includes such information as name, address, telephone, date and place of birth, major field of study, participation in official athletics, weight and height of team members, dates of attendance, degrees and awards, and most recent institution attended. The institution is then supposed to allow "reasonable" time for a parent or student to indicate that some or all of this information should not be released—an unlisted telephone number, for instance.

A parental or student request for access must be granted "within a reasonable period," but never more than forty-five days after the request. "Access" includes both inspection of the record and copying of documents, the latter at a fee not exceeding the actual cost of reproduction. Where a record contains information on more than one student, the institution may reveal only information pertaining to the requesting student; if physical inspection of the record in such a case would violate the privacy of other students, the institution may simply "inform" the student of the contents of the record.

There may be some controversy over the proposed regulations granting the right to make copies, as it has been argued that this might place students and parents under pressure from outsiders to copy and hand over records which would not otherwise be available to them. The argument has some merit, and, as in the matter of waivers, vigilance will be required to assure that students are not coerced into ceding their right to privacy as the price of a job, credit rating, or security clearance. However, experience has shown that the right merely to see the record may not be sufficient, particularly if its contents are voluminous or complex. Memory often does not serve faithfully; then too, a former student or a parent is not always on the spot to make a personal inspection of the records. If a problem of coercion does arise, it will have to be met directly, not by a diminution of the student's own right of access.

The proposed regulations warn that the right of access may not be thwarted by destruction of records. If a student or parent demands to see a file, it may not then be destroyed as a way of circumventing the demand. On the other hand, it was observed during the congressional debate that the destruction of some records might be a good thing; the fewer the records kept, the fewer the opportunities for abuse, especially when the data include anecdotal material, subjective judgments, and unverified complaints. But again, precipitate destruction of such material which has already been circulated to outsiders can be of more harm than help to the student by making it impossible to discover derogatory information that may have been used earlier. Some privacy advocates have argued that the schools should be under an affirmative duty to notify a student whenever any seriously adverse information goes into his or her records.

Challenges and Hearings

Students have the right to make "reasonable requests" to the institution for an explanation and interpretation of documents in their records. Notations which appear to be "inaccurate, misleading, or otherwise inappropriate" may be challenged. If in the course of informal discussions the institution refuses to correct or delete the challenged information, or to enter an explanatory statement by the parent or student, there may be a hearing on the merits of the dispute.

The act's provisions for challenge and hearings caused

great consternation in the educational community. The alarm was raised that schools would be forced to hold hearings to justify "why Johnny got a B instead of an A." This was not what the act's authors intended. Hearings might indeed be required if Johnny claims that his professor really did give him an A and that the office records are incorrect, but not merely to satisfy Johnny's or his parents' belief that he *should* have had an A. One would hope that institutions will be glad to correct their records upon the presentation of evidence that the records are wrong. Or, if a child has been placed in a special class for slow learners, the parents might consult outside professional advice to review the evidence upon which the school has acted, and perhaps be able to show the school that its evidence is misleading or inaccurate. And one would also hope that an institution will be only too happy to erase unsubstantiated accusations or derogatory comments when the student is able to show that they are "misleading" or "inappropriate." The school stands to benefit no less than the student from having fair, accurate, and timely records.

The act does not specify what form the hearings must take. The HEW regulations require that a hearing be held at the request of either party, that the institution publish its hearing procedures, that the hearing be conducted by an official of the institution or other party not having a "direct interest" in the outcome. This last provision could prove troublesome, as it can be argued that any school official has a very real interest in defending the institution against challenges. The hearing must be held "within a reasonable time" after it has been requested, parents and students must have a "full and fair opportunity" to present their evidence, and a decision must be announced "within a reasonable time."

Consent to Release of Records

The opportunity to review and correct one's records is but one half of an effective right to privacy. The other half is the ability to control the release of information to outsiders. The Buckley Act requires institutions to obtain the written consent of parents or eligible students before releasing student records to outside parties.

There are a number of exceptions to the consent requirement. Personally identifiable information may be released without consent to the following:

1. Teachers and other officials of the same institution, including any of its component parts (such as colleges within a university), who "have legitimate educational interests"

2. Officials of another school in which the student is seeking enrollment. In such a case the parents must be notified that the records are being transferred, must receive copies on request, and must be accorded opportunity for a hearing to challenge the contents of the records before they are transferred.

3. Specified state and federal authorities engaged in the audit, evaluation, and enforcement of federally supported educational programs

4. In connection with a student's application for or receipt of financial aid

5. State or local officials authorized by state statutes adopted *before* 19 November 1974 to receive such information

6. Outside organizations (the Educational Testing Service and College Entrance Examination Board, for example) conducting studies for developing or administering predictive tests, administering student aid programs, or improving instruction

7. Accrediting organizations

8. Parents of "dependent students" as defined by the Internal Revenue Code. Colleges, therefore, may send a dependent student's grades to his or her parents without the student's consent, and must do so on the parent's request.

Finally, information may be released without consent to "appropriate persons" in an "emergency" where necessary "to protect the health or safety of the student or other persons." Congress and HEW warned that this exception must be narrowly interpreted, lest "health and safety" become merely a convenient password for circumventing the intent of the act. Where a student is thought to be on the verge of suicide, however, or a serious epidemic has broken out on campus, it may be necessary to invoke this provision.

Consent by a parent or eligible student to the release of records must be written, signed, and dated, specifying the records to be released, the persons designated to receive them, and the purpose for which they are to be used. The parent or student must be given a copy of the records on request. The receiving party may not permit anyone else to have access to the records without a further written authorization.

The school is required to keep a record of all persons and organizations requesting access to a student's records (except for requests by teachers or officials within the institution itself) and a specific indication of their legitimate interest in obtaining information in each case. It must keep this record with the student's other education records and must allow parents and eligible students to inspect it. The only other persons who may see this record are the school officials responsible for maintaining the files and those school and governmental officials involved in implementing and enforcing the act.

Sanctions

The act's principal sanction is money. Federal funds can be withheld from any institution which violates the act.

The HEW proposals establish an HEW office and review board to handle complaints of violations of the act. A complaint must be filed in writing within 180 days of the alleged violation. After the submission of evidence and arguments by both parties, HEW will announce its findings and, if it finds the institution at fault, will specify what it must do to comply with the act. If the school still does not comply, a review board can begin proceedings for the withholding of federal funds. The Secretary of HEW is permitted to grant a waiver of compliance for a "reasonable" period in those jurisdictions where existing state or local laws may conflict with the Buckley Act. The waiver is meant only to grant the legislatures time to bring their laws into compliance with federal law.

The special HEW office established to enforce the Buckley Act is under the direction of Thomas S. McFee, at Room 5660, Department of Health, Education, and Welfare, 330 Independence Avenue, S.W., Washington, D.C. 20201; telephone 202-245-7488.

The Buckley Act is not a perfect piece of legislation, but it is a pretty good one. Students and their parents, and former students as well, should take full advantage of their rights under the act, undeterred by any signs of reluctance or resistance by school administrations. In fact, there is no reason to doubt that most schools will comply, provided that students and parents are well informed about their rights and willing to assert them with determination. ACLU's affiliates will stand ready to advise and assist those whose rights under the Buckly Act are denied.

PRIVACY VERSUS THE PRESS [6]

The right to privacy—perhaps the most cherished right of all—is guaranteed, but more and more lately it is coming into conflict in the courts with the press's First Amendment right to report freely news. . . . [On March 3, 1975] the Supreme Court ruled, in a rape case, that newspapers and radio stations could not be subjected to either criminal prosecution or civil damage suits for reporting accurate information available from law enforcement records. But only

[6] From "Privacy vs. the Press: The Issue Remains,' by Martin Arnold, staff news analyst. New York *Times*. p 12. Mr. 6, '75. © 1975 by The New York Times Company. Reprinted by permission.

time and more cases will tell how broadly the court intended
to apply that ruling.

Courts have generally held over the last several decades
that public figures, such as politicians, entertainers and athletes, give up their right to privacy in return for being public figures. The question remains: How much privacy does
a person who is not a public figure have when his privacy
collides with the rights of the press?

The press's right to disseminate information was ex-
plicity guaranteed in the Constitution; and an individual's
right to privacy has been obtained through a series of judicial rulings, each one put atop the other like so many
bricks in a wall, since the beginning of the century.

Two Broad Categories

Briefly, there are two broad categories of cases involving
privacy vs. the press's right to print news. One involves what
is called depicting a person in a "false light"—this is close
to but separate from libel law—and the other involves the
public disclosure of private facts about private persons. . . .

[The March 3] Supreme Court ruling pertained to the
latter category. The high court, in an 8-to-1 decision, struck
down a Georgia law that made it a misdemeanor to print or
broadcast the name of a rape victim. Several other states
have similar laws. It was the first time that the Court had
been asked to rule that an individual's right to privacy
could outweigh the First Amendment when the news report
was true.

The case was brought by the father of a young woman
who had been raped and killed in 1971 by six teen-age boys.
The father sought damages from an Atlanta television station for invasion of privacy for broadcasting his daughter's
name. The Georgia courts upheld the father as a matter of
law, and the television station appealed to the Supreme
Court.

The Court ruled that "once true information is disclosed

in public court documents open to public inspection, the press cannot be sanctioned for publishing it."

Ruling Restricted

The Court then dampened the ruling somewhat by saying that it was confining the ruling to "the narrower interface between press and privacy" involved in printing the name of a rape victim rather than "the broader question whether truthful publications may ever be subjected to civil or criminal liability."

Still, the reality of the law is such that lawyers who defend newspapers in privacy cases will now bring appeals based on the broader words of the ruling, hoping finally to inch the Court toward absolutely guaranteeing the press the right to print whatever information it wants. It probably will take many more cases, involving crimes other than rape, to determine how far the Court is willing to go.

The aim of the press and its lawyers is to get the courts eventually to apply what is called "the Sullivan Standard" to privacy cases involving people who are not public figures.

In the landmark case of *The New York Times Company v. Sullivan,* the high court held that a public figure could not recover damages from a newspaper in a libel case unless the plaintiff established "clear and convincing" proof that the statement published was false, and that the publication either knew it was false or that it acted in "reckless disregard" to what should have been its "high degree of awareness of probable falsity." This is an extremely tough standard for a plaintiff to meet in court.

Between the *Times-Sullivan* ruling and . . . [the March 3d] ruling, there have been a number of cases involving privacy vs. the press, but most lawyers who specialize in such cases do not believe that the rulings have been broad enough to substantially clear the murky waters. . . .

[In December 1974] for instance, the Court ruled, in a "false light" case, against the press; therefore, the laws of right of privacy were not modified by that decision.

Children Interviewed

The case involved a construction worker in West Virginia who was one of forty-four persons killed in the collapse of a bridge in 1967. Five months after the accident, a reporter and a photographer from the Cleveland *Plain Dealer* visited the home of the worker's widow while she was at work and interviewed and photographed her children.

The resulting article referred to the family as "hillbillies," depicted them as victims of the public's neglect of Appalachia, and said the widow refused to discuss the family's problems. The newspaper later admitted that the woman had not been interviewed. She sued, and was awarded $60,000 in damages.

The paper appealed to the Supreme Court, arguing that it had a right to report freely about people involved in such a dramatic event as the collapse of a bridge, and that in this case it had done so without culpable malice or recklessness. That was the issue, as far as the press was concerned: Do private people who are connected to events of public interest have a buffer of privacy against reporting and, if so, how wide a buffer?

The Court ruled that the family was subjected to "calculated falsehoods" and that the "jury was plainly justified" in finding that the family had been depicted "in a false light through knowing or reckless untruth."

There are other privacy cases pending in which the press has an interest. In Houston, for instance, the Houston *Chronicle* has sought a state court injunction against the police department's selectively denying the news media access to both formal and informal arrest records and offense reports. The police contend that they may deny access because, they say, it involves an unjustified invasion of privacy.

The *Chronicle* is appealing. [A decision has been handed down permitting the press free access to offense reports and stipulating that the city may selectively decide upon access to criminal records. The filing of an appeal is under consideration.—Ed.] So with all these cases . . . the Supreme Court has still not answered in general terms that very subtle question of which is more important, the privacy of the individual or the privilege of the press. Most legal experts think it will be a slow process to define the distinction between private facts and public news, and to determine precisely when the printing of a private fact is offensive.

PRIVACY OF PRESIDENTS [7]

George Wallace is a paraplegic, but he insists he's completely up to the physical demands of the presidency. Is he really?

Hubert Humphrey, who's suddenly moved back to the top of Democratic presidential speculation, was getting X-ray therapy two years ago for a small tumor on the lining of his bladder. Now, at age sixty-four, he says he's never been fitter. Is he really?

If Nelson Rockefeller is nominated and elected to a full vice presidential term, he'll be sixty-eight on Inauguration Day. Aides report him as full of beans as ever. Is he really?

It's time to stop tiptoeing around the question of the candidate's age and health. It's time to start talking about these matters, and to keep on talking and asking questions about them all through the coming year.

In fact, it's time to urge, or even require, that our candidates for high office submit to a thorough examination by independent medical experts.

Admittedly, the whole subject isn't an easy one to treat. Discussing it can seem to be bad form, ghoulish, sick. But it's a vital subject, one which, if ignored or made light of, could easily come back to haunt us.

The nation has gone through enough traumas in recent years: One President assassinated, another President and a

[7] From "No More Tiptoeing," by Alan L. Otten, staff correspondent, Washington, D.C. *Wall Street Journal*. p 10. S. 4, '75. Reprinted with permission of *The Wall Street Journal* © 1975 Dow Jones & Company, Inc. All Rights Reserved.

Vice President forced from office, a vice presidential nomi-
nee revealed to have been treated for mental depression.
Some such shocks can't be anticipated and avoided, but the
risks of advanced age or ill health can at least be noted, discussed, weighed. And while the matter is most critical when
it involves presidential or vice presidential candidates, it
also applies to would-be Senators, Representatives, gov-
ernors.

The health cover-up problem isn't a new one, of course.
Woodrow Wilson's wife and doctor kept from the public
the fact that Mr. Wilson was almost totally incapacitated
during his last nine months in the presidency. Franklin D.
Roosevelt's deteriorating health was carefully screened from
voters when he last ran in 1944. The public still doesn't
really know just what health problems John F. Kennedy
had in the White House and what medication he was taking.

A Touchy Subject

In some ways, age may be touchier to talk about than
health. There are more old people around, and many an
oldster is obviously considerably spryer and sharper than
most of his juniors.

Yet the risks of electing older people are overwhelmingly
clear. Mortality tables assure us that older people are more
likely to die than younger ones. There is good reason why
so many companies, colleges and other organizations require
their executives to retire at sixty-five.

Most older people do slow down in their mental and
physical reactions. They become more set in their ways—
inflexible, crotchety, cantankerous. Congress is full of people
who would meet most medical definitions of senility. . . .

If age is a problem in Congress, it's an even greater worry
in the White House, where responsibility is less easily
delegated or shared. Mr. Rockefeller may be as sharp as
ever, but there are at least a few who find his attention span
shortening, his energy ebbing more often, his reactions tend-
ing to be a little more temperamental.

Mr. Rockefeller isn't the only sexagenarian in the race for President or Vice President. Mr. Ford is almost a youngster; come Inauguration Day, he will be a mere sixty-three. The seemingly youthful Ronald Reagan will be sixty-five. Henry Jackson will be sixty-four, Edmund Muskie sixty-two, Mr. Humphrey sixty-five. (Dwight Eisenhower, perhaps surprisingly to those who recall him as he was towards the end of his presidency, was only sixty-two when he took office.)

Age is, however, at least an easily determined fact, one that people can readily discover and judge for themselves. (And judge they do: More old-timers are being voted out of Congress, and most politicians now believe that obvious advanced age is a definite political liability.) But ill health, physical or psychic, is far harder to detect and assess.

Mr. Wallace's situation is much in point. His staff says he's as healthy as most people, his mind keener than ever. Visiting reporters can watch him work out on the parallel bars. Political backers cite FDR's wheel-chair campaigning.

Yet all that's more than a little misleading. Mr. Roosevelt's legs were weak but not completely useless, as Mr. Wallace's are. Mr. Roosevelt suffered his illness at a far younger age, and doctors generally believe that a younger person can better build compensating resources and strengths. Mr. Wallace does, for instance, tire easily.

Doctors also pretty well agree that all paraplegics are prone to urinary tract infections, particularly when, as is the case with Mr. Wallace, the person has no control over bowels or bladder and thus can't eliminate waste. In a detailed article recently in the *Village Voice,* Ann Pincus reports that Mr. Wallace has had three urinary tract infections in the past six months; that these and other afflictions have required such extensive use of antibiotics that his body may be becoming immune to antibiotics, and thus less able to combat a future infection; that he is in almost constant pain and three times a day takes a powerful pain-killing drug that can have serious side effects (though not habit-forming or mind-affecting); and that he still has periods of

deep depression. In addition, Mrs. Pincus notes—as does anyone who's seen Mr. Wallace over a period of years—that his
long-time hearing difficulties are getting steadily worse.

So how are the voters supposed to find out and evaluate
the health of Mr. Wallace and his fellow-hopefuls? One
idea—perhaps an imperfect one but also perhaps the best
available—would require some sort of independent physical
and psychiatric examination of candidates for the higher
political offices.

Right now, there's either no examination at all, or an
examination by the candidate's doctors that is taken with
more than a little salt by a public grown used to being lied
to. The Nixon White House, for instance, issued fairly
detailed reports on the President's fight against phlebitis—
but no one knew where medical accuracy stopped and
political public relations took over.

The Privacy Objection

The American Medical Association, civil libertarians
and others resist the idea of a compulsory health examination as an invasion of personal privacy. The AMA's Principles of Medical Ethics stipulate that a doctor can disclose
health information to the press only if specifically authorized by the person involved. The privacy objection, though,
seems naive and irrelevant.

Every candidate automatically gives up most rights to
privacy, and the political system already invades privacy
to a great degree. A candidate must disclose campaign
financing details; there are investigations into his private
income, and there are even, as Mrs. Ford discovered, questions about an offspring's love life.

The searching eye of television and the gossip reports
of political columnists often raise health questions that are
better disposed of authoritatively. And, most importantly,
the question of the candidate's privacy must be weighed
against the broader public good; medical examinations are

now required for many private jobs—why not for the most important public ones?

Openness on health issues might be novel but it's not completely unprecedented. Back in the 1950s, White House Press Secretary James Hagerty's bulletins about President Eisenhower's illnesses were almost revolting in their medical detail. President Johnson's health problems were similarly set forth.

There are also ways to limit invasion of health privacy. Dr. John Sonneland, a Spokane surgeon who is on the board of Common Cause and is an advocate of the independent health examination points out that the testing could be done in a clinic or other large institution where some degree of anonymity is preserved. Broad ground rules could be set by medical societies. Doctors could omit medical history that doesn't bear on the candidate's suitability for the job, reporting publicly only what is relevant.

To be sure, there are real difficulties in the whole idea. It's easier, for example, to agree on physical disability than on mental disability. Yet there are batteries of tests that are reasonably objective, and doctors use these every day to diagnose illnesses of both types. In any event, their verdict wouldn't be automatically throwing people off the ballot, but merely laying the facts before the public.

Obviously, the mere fact of a serious prior illness or of advanced age shouldn't rule out a candidate. People who are paraplegic or who have been treated for cancer go on to live active, productive lives. Quite a few sixty-five-year olds are more than up to any job. Most people who get psychiatric help are stronger individuals as a result.

But let's at least get these things out into the open, examine them closely, and think about them carefully. Let's stop pretending the problems aren't there or don't matter. Too much depends on the answer.

ON BALANCING RIGHTS[8]

The preservation of privacy seems to be one of the main legislative passions of the moment—a passion in part created out of congressional reaction to public indignation over the Watergate disclosures. Obviously this concern for privacy is welcome—as long as it isn't used as an excuse to strengthen the opportunities for secrecy in the government. It should come as no surprise, in the present climate, that legislation has been and probably will again be considered by Congress that in the name of privacy would forbid access by the press to such traditionally public records as police blotters and criminal records. The framers of this legislation have been aware that there are problems in this approach, and have tried to solve them.

As an example of what can result from laws intending to protect individual privacy, Honolulu last summer [1974] turned into a police city for a few days, until the courts intervened. A statute designed to protect the privacy of arrested persons had been passed by the state legislature. It was interpreted by police officials as prohibiting the release to journalists of any information about incarcerations or arrests. In effect, the press could not find out who was in jail for what offense—all in the name of protecting the rights of individuals. Citing the same law, a prosecutor refused to release names of persons indicted by a grand jury.

The intent of this privacy legislation was to prevent the careless bandying about of names of individuals arrested; the effect, as the law was applied by government, was to cut off the flow of information to the public about police activities—information that must be available if the rights of due process and of a speedy trial are to be preserved.

[8] From "Secrecy, Privacy, and Publicity," by W. H. Hornby, vice-president and executive editor of the Denver *Post*, chairman of the Freedom of Information Committee of the American Society of Newspaper Editors. *Columbia Journalism Review*. 13:10-11. Mr./Ap. '75. © 1975 Graduate School of Journalism, Columbia University. Reprinted by permission.

We still need to know who is in jail and what the charges
are against them. We still need to know who has been indicted. If we don't insist on this knowledge, we are in the
same position as the Germans who, in their privacy, won-
dered about the sighing cargoes of those long freight trains
that passed in the night. My point, simply, is this: our
passion for privacy in this age of great worry about individualism can easily be directed into unwholesome channels by
those interested in the cause of official secrecy.

Balancing Privacy, Secrecy, and Publicity

Edward Shils, a sociologist, political scientist, and a student of the American, British, and German systems of
government, has written of the balance we seek. Reviewing
the history of Western man's struggle for freedom in *The
Torment of Secrecy*, he writes:

The struggle for constitutional government, for the extension
of the franchise, and particularly for the freedom of the press . . .
was directed against privacy in government. Almost as much as
the extension of the franchise and constitutional restraint on
monarchial absolutism, publicity regarding political and administrative affairs was a fundamental aim of the modern liberal democratic movement. The demand for the publicity of governmental affairs was attended by a demand for the protection and
reinforcement of privacy in other spheres—a demand which was
itself the child of the aspiration for individual liberty.

The result, Shils says, was a balancing of rights.

The tradition of liberal, individualistic democracy maintained
an equilibrium of publicity, privacy, and secrecy. The equilibrium
was enabled to exist as long as the beneficiaries and protagonists
of each sector . . . respected the legitimacy of the other two and
were confident that they would not use their power and opportunities to disrupt the equilibrium. The principles of privacy, secrecy, and publicity are not harmonious among themselves. The
existence of each rests on a self-restrictive tendency in each of
the others.

In these definitions, we should note, publicity is a short-
hand expression for the free flow of information held vital

to the democratic political process. Publicity simply means the freedom of the press in its broadest interpretation. Privacy, of course, is the right of the individual to be let alone, to enjoy solitude, intimacy, reasonable anonymity, and to reserve personal information. And secrecy really means official secrecy—the right of the government to withhold information.

Each of these elements is necessary to some degree, but what is the balance between them? These are the very questions the country agonized over during the impeachment debate: when can publicity expose secrecy? When can secrecy invade privacy?

Few can doubt, surely, that these elements are getting out of balance, with the passion for official secrecy overriding both the right of the individual to privacy and the right of the citizen to free access to essential information about the actions of his government.

Shils wrote during the McCarthy era [1951-1954], when Congress, rather than the President, was equating the sanctity of governmental secrecy with national security, and was ruthlessly invading the privacy of individuals [by the activities of the committee chaired by Senator Joseph McCarthy (Republican, Wisconsin), investigating subversive influences in government—Ed.]. The Congress gradually corrected its own excess, and censured Senator McCarthy.

Now, two decades later, the Nixon Administration has met a similar fate, in large part because of its passion for secrecy—maintained all too often at the expense of individual privacy as well as the public's right to know what its elected officials are up to.

Out of the McCarthy era came an overblown system of classification and repression of public information. Out of the Watergate era, similarly, may come legislation and executive rulings in the name of privacy which in fact advance secrecy and penalize legitimate publicity. In my judgment, the clear measure of the shifting balance over these decades is that secrecy already has advanced too far.

Regaining a Balance Against Secrecy

The real issue is not between privacy and publicity, but between both privacy and publicity allied in the fight to regain their balance against secrecy.

Many critics of journalism think differently. They maintain that the worst invaders of privacy are newspapers, magazines, and broadcasters. One reason for this impression is the relative visibility and noisiness of journalism. The governmental war against privacy, on the contrary, is carried on quietly, in the name of "national interest" or "national security." Watergate has revealed just a few of the many invasions of privacy conducted by government in the name of national security. These tendencies can be found under all forms of government. But they reach their ultimate expression in totalitarian societies, where governmental secrecy and the lack of privacy accorded to individuals approach the absolute—the literal negative of the libertarian aims of our own Constitution.

When compared to invasions of privacy practiced by governments in the name of secrecy, the cases of irresponsible intrusions by journalists into the privacy of individuals, however inexcusable, shrink to a regrettable but relatively small proportion. These cases are publicly litigated, and most privacy law is written around them. These battles are carried on in the open, and we witness them. We tend therefore to think of them as being the whole war. They are not. A journalistic invasion of privacy may affront dignity and might damage someone financially, but such journalistic abuses seldom tend to destroy liberty itself. I suspect that Alexander Solzhenitsyn, for example, preferred to endure occasional invasions of his privacy by journalists rather than forever surrender all his privacy to government.

V. TOWARD GREATER PRIVACY

EDITOR'S INTRODUCTION

There are many indications the recent congressional, presidential, and citizen interest in privacy will lead to new legislation and to further curbing of invasions by both government and business. It is these aspects that are discussed in this closing section.

The future implications of the Privacy Act of 1974 have yet to be fully spelled out. Doubtless further legislation will follow. The act's provisions and suggested legislation are reviewed by Constance Holden, an editorial staff writer for *Science*.

What the newly established White House Domestic Council Committee on the Right of Privacy has already undertaken and what it proposes to investigate are sketched by Douglas W. Metz, acting executive director, and George B. Trubow, general counsel, of the Committee.

Two United States Senators, concerned activists in this area, Henry M. Jackson (Democrat, Washington) and Gaylord Nelson (Democrat, Wisconsin), next comment on the present state of privacy legislation and on continued privacy invasions that need curbing. Both Senators outline legislation they feel is needed.

In 1974 the Roscoe Pound–American Trial Lawyers Foundation held a conference on privacy in a free society. A synopsis of the conference's complete findings prepared by Richard S. Jacobson, editor of *Trial* magazine, is included as the last article in this compilation.

FRUITFUL PRIVACY EFFORTS OF CONGRESS [1]

The issue of privacy is finally having its day in Congress. The last Congress (93d) saw the introduction of scores of bills designed to protect individuals from surveillance and record-keeping activity of government and government-funded agencies.

Two of them passed. One was the so-called Buckley amendment to the Elementary and Secondary Education Amendments of 1974, which increases access to student records by students and their parents, and inhibits it for others. [For further information see "Student Privacy Rights," in Section IV above.] The other, more far-reaching law represents the first attempt to set governmentwide standards regulating data banks containing records on individuals held by most agencies in the federal government. Called the Privacy Act of 1974 [cosponsored by Senator Henry M. Jackson of Washington], it is the final legacy of Senator Sam J. Ervin (Democrat, North Carolina) who retired from Congress . . . [in December 1974]. The law goes into effect on 27 September [1975].

These two measures are the early blossomings of what promises to be an entirely new family of legislation designed to stem the real or potential erosion of personal liberty caused by massive and promiscuous data collection, use, and dissemination by all levels of government as well as the private sector.

The Privacy Act is couched in fairly general terms—what it does is articulate a set of principles to ensure that information is only used for the purpose for which it was collected and to let members of the public know what the government knows about them. It lays a basis for future, more specific legislation governing the handling of various categories of information. The law is actually one of the

[1] From "Privacy: Congressional Efforts Are Coming to Fruition," by Constance Holden, editorial staff member. *Science*. 88:713-14. My. 16, '75. Copyright 1975 by the American Association for the Advancement of Science. Reprinted with permission.

federal government's first steps in building a theoretical framework for achieving a balance, in both the public and private sectors, between the individual's right to privacy and society's "need to know." The latter concept is already formalized in the Freedom of Information [FOI] Act; one intended effect of the privacy measure is to clarify one of the exemptions in the FOI act that prohibits the dispensation of information when that involves a clearly unwarranted invasion of privacy.

There is a fair amount of stabbing in the dark involved in privacy legislation, and it is case law that will eventually determine its substance. Meanwhile, as Ruth M. Davis, director of the Institute for Computer Sciences and Technology at the National Bureau of Standards [NBS], observes, one inevitable spinoff will be the development and revival of good information management practices. (NBS has been deeply involved in developing standards for confidentiality and security in automated data systems.) The government has been in possession of files it didn't even know about, as was revealed in a three-year study completed in 1974 by the Ervin subcommittee of the Senate Judiciary Committee. That study found 858 data banks in 54 agencies, all of which contained more than 1.25 billion files on individuals. The Privacy Act should make it more difficult to maintain the large number of obsolete, redundant, or unnecessary files that number would seem to imply.

Over the years, legal scholars have attempted to define privacy—one of the earliest is Louis D. Brandeis's formulation of it in 1890 as "the right to be let alone." A later formulation by [Professor] Alan F. Westin of Columbia University is that privacy is "the claim of individuals, groups or institutions to determine for themselves when, how and to what extent information about themselves is communicated to others." Privacy is not defined by the Constitution, although the preponderance of legal opinion has it that the right to privacy is implicit in the Bill of Rights.

Congress and Privacy

Since the substance of privacy cannot be strictly defined, Congress has chosen instead to establish procedures which enable individuals to take measures to protect what they perceive to be their privacy.

The 1974 act is the first federal statute to establish this right. How did it finally get through? Considerable public interest became focused on the subject during a long-running series of hearings held by former Representative Cornelius Gallagher's (Democrat, New Jersey) select privacy committee during the 1960s. One development that brought attention to bear on privacy was a proposal by the then Bureau of the Budget to set up a centralized, automated National Data Bank. The idea was that efficiency would be served by pooling the files of such mammoth information-holders as the Internal Revenue Service, the Social Security Administration, and the Census Bureau. It seemed like a good idea until critics pointed up the unsavory, not to mention frightening, implications of thousands of bureaucrats having fingertip access to cradle-to-grave information on millions of Americans. The proposal was quashed.

The civil disorders and law-and-order ethos of the 1960s probably slowed the march of privacy legislation, but as citizens found themselves increasingly numbered and coded and categorized—not just criminals and poor people, but ordinary types who minded their own business—the image of the country being taken over by a heedless army of computers has come even closer to the surface of public consciousness. Watergate greatly increased the sense of urgency. Ironically enough, with Watergate in high tide, Nixon gave his new Vice President Gerald Ford the go-ahead to chair a new Committee on the Right of Privacy within the White House Domestic Council. Official history has it that Ford was a little nonplussed by the investigative procedures that preceded his appointment as Vice President and developed a permanent personal interest in privacy matters. His suc-

cessor, Nelson Rockefeller, has not displayed any notable
involvement in the committee's activities, but the committee, directed by former management consultant executive
Douglas Metz, has by all accounts done an admirable job
working with Congress and generally giving the privacy
issue high-level visibility and support. In Congress, a coalition of two usually divergent factions—the conservatives and
the civil libertarians—has created a base broad enough to
boost privacy proposals into law. In the Senate this has been
exemplified by [Sam] Ervin and Roman Hruska (Republican, Nebraska) joining forces; in the House, by the coauthor-
ship of several privacy bills by liberal Edward I. Koch (Democrat, New York) and conservative Barry Goldwater Jr.
(Republican, California).

The 1974 Privacy Act

The Privacy Act was originally framed to cover information-handling practices by state and local governments and
private industry as well as the federal government. It was
subsequently pared down to apply only to the federal government, and even there large areas—notably criminal justice information systems—are left out. But it does set down
unprecedented principles that will presumably be drawn
upon in the creation of future privacy laws at every level of
government.

The principles are taken from a proposed code of fair
information practices contained in a 1973 report called
Records, Computers, and the Rights of Citizens put together
by the Advisory Committee on Automated Personal Data
Systems of the Department of Health, Education, and Welfare. That report asserted that there must be no personal
data record-keeping systems whose very existence is secret;
that individuals must be allowed to find out what's in their
files and to cause erroneous information to be corrected;
that agencies should make clear the purposes of their data
systems; and that information collected for one purpose

must not be used for another without the consent of the data subject.

The Privacy Act requires that all federal agencies publish annual reports on the nature of all their personal data-keeping systems and obtain permission for expansion of data systems or creation of new ones. Interagency transfer of information is tightly restricted except for what is called "routine use" (defined in the law as "compatible with the purpose for which it was collected"). The law sets up a Privacy Protection Study Commission to monitor enforcement of the statute [which is administered by the Office of Management and Budget (OMB)] and to study issues that will have to be dealt with in the future. It will study, for example, the spread of the use of the Social Security number for purposes unrelated to Social Security—a phenomenon that, while convenient for record keepers, makes it easier for various files on an individual to be integrated with each other.

The law is vague—the OMB has issued a 114-page document of guidelines for its implementation—and it will probably take several years and countless court cases to define its substance and workability. One reason for the vagueness is that it is more of a preventive or anticipatory measure than one to curtail specific abuses. It is easy to collect horror stories involving misuse of private information—but the most pervasive abuses are more subtle, more difficult to track down, and often perpetrated by agencies whose intentions are of the best.

No one really knows how expensive it will be to implement the new law, although a Senate staffer says the OMB's estimate of $200 million to $300 million a year is a gross exaggeration, particularly in light of the fact that some savings are bound to be effected by the correction of sloppy information-handling practices.

What Future for Privacy Legislation?

The next generation of congressional privacy legislation is now being designed to fill in the gaps left by the Privacy Act and to develop rules, by subject area, for information systems operated or funded by the federal government.

Most important on this year's agenda [1975] is a law to regulate the handling of criminal justice information by the federal government and all state and local law enforcement agencies that get federal funds. The House and Senate judiciary committees now have two bills under consideration, one authored by the Administration and one masterminded by [Sam] Ervin. There is general agreement that criminal justice files are pretty much in disarray. On the federal level, it is difficult to place restrictions on information management because the Federal Bureau of Investigation (FBI) doesn't want any rules—such as sealing criminal histories or expunging arrest records after a specified period of time—that would cramp pursuit of its mission. The problems are legion. Lack of accuracy and completeness of records is one of the worst. It is estimated, for example, that of the arrest records held by the FBI's National Crime Information Center (a data bank in which states voluntarily participate), 70 percent contain no information on the final disposition of the cases.

The spread of automation has allowed for easy and indiscriminate circulation of arrest records (whether or not followed by conviction) and unverified data. What's more, prospective employers, credit agencies, and other non-law-enforcement bodies are given access to individual criminal records. The bills pending are designed to limit the use of incomplete records, to keep criminal justice information within the system, and to inhibit direct access of one system into another. And, in keeping with the Privacy Act (into which the final measure is supposed to plug), subjects of criminal files would have the opportunity to inspect and demand correction of their files.

There are quite a few other privacy bills simmering along in various committees governing use of Internal Revenue Service files, government personnel files, medical files, banking and savings and loan files, military surveillance, and so on.

Senator William Proxmire (Democrat, Wisconsin) intends to introduce amendments to the Fair Credit Reporting Act. That act, passed in 1970, was the government's pioneer effort at giving individuals some control over personal information by requiring that consumer credit agencies tell them what is in their files. The act is now deemed inadequate, and provisions are being drawn up that would enable people to see their files in person, uncover specific reasons why they were rejected for credit, learn the identity of their "accusers," and take legal action on broader grounds than those allowed in the original act.

There is also a bill, introduced by [Representatives] Koch and Goldwater and named, appropriately enough, H.R. 1984, that would apply, to data banks held by local governments and the private sector, the same principles that the Privacy Act establishes for those within the federal government. [This bill, called the Comprehensive Right to Privacy Act, is still pending in the Judiciary Committee.—Ed.] The Administration thinks such a measure would be premature, and many private businesses contend that specific abuses should be identified before the government starts tinkering with their information systems. There certainly would seem to be a need to sharpen up definitions. What, for example, is a personal file? What, for that matter, is a data bank? Some people fear that such a law could even put restrictions on the maintenance of newspaper morgues or company correspondence files. Anyway, H.R. 1984's chance of passage, at least in its present form, is extremely remote.

It may be that the states will take the responsibility for laws governing privacy in the private sector. Several states, including Massachusetts, California, and Hawaii, are developing laws governing their own data systems; farthest along is Minnesota, which now has a law governing data banks containing personal information held by all states and state-funded agencies. Some private organizations are moving ahead on their own—IBM, for example, has developed new measures to limit the scope of information required for employee files, and is advertising principles it has adopted to give employees access to their own records and limit access by third parties. If the trend continues, privacy practices could become formally embodied in the structures of large organizations in the way equal employment opportunity functions have been.

A new family of privacy legislation will mean a new family of trade-offs. The most fundamental question relates to the amount of information the government needs on individuals in order to protect the well-being of society. If future laws put limits on the amount, type, retention, and use of information collected from individuals, there will inevitably be new impediments to efficient rendering of government services, law enforcement, and the availability of data for statistical and research purposes. Balanced against these drawbacks will be not only the indefinable "right to privacy" but also the feeling of freedom and security that enables citizens to exercise their constitutional rights without looking over their shoulders all the time.

THE COMPLEXITY OF PRIVACY [2]

The White House Domestic Council Committee on the Right of Privacy was established in February 1974 to study individual privacy and the collection of personal data.

There is presently no coherent body of "privacy law," but rather an amalgam of legal concepts deriving from the

[2] From article by Douglas W. Metz and George B. Trubow, acting executive director and general counsel, respectively, of the White House Domestic Council on the Right of Privacy. *Trial.* 11:13+. Ja./F. '75. Reprinted by permission of *Trial* magazine © 1974, published bi-monthly by The Association of Trial Lawyers of America. All rights reserved.

Constitution and various interests recognized by the common law.

The confidentiality of personal information is perhaps the central privacy issue, and thus the Privacy Committee has devoted much of its effort to studying information and record-keeping practices. If an agency or business has information references on an individual, what responsibility accompanies the stewardship of that information?

The principles for fair information practices established by the Department of Health, Education, and Welfare are good guidelines to follow:

1. Save in limited areas of national security, there should be no personal data system whose very existence is secret.

2. Individuals should have the right to look at files that contain personal information about them.

3. Agencies that use personal information should take care not to collect and keep more than they need for their purpose, and the information should be accurate and reasonably current and complete, depending on the nature of use.

4. Information should be used only for the purposes for which it was gathered, unless the data subject gives consent to some other use.

5. There should be simple procedures by which the data subject can see to it that outdated, erroneous or incomplete information is amended or corrected.

6. Personal data should be safeguarded against unauthorized access and improper use.

The first five points go to confidentiality and information practices; the sixth point addresses security of data systems. These principles have been generally accepted by the Privacy Committee and form the basis for the work that is under way. The questions surrounding matters of privacy and information confidentiality are many and complex. As President Ford stated in his capacity as Chairman of the Privacy Committee:

In our zeal to protect this right more adequately, we should not attempt to remedy all abuses within the four corners of one bill. Potential intrusions on personal privacy have too many facets and the public interests involved are too complex to permit all-inclusive remedies. The burden of legislating in this field requires a delicate balancing of the interests of each individual to control the gathering and use of information about him and the interests of government in obtaining the information needed to administer its services and enforce its laws.

The committee realizes that the bulk of privacy and confidentiality concerns are within the domain of state and local government and the private sector. Though there are 2.8 million federal civilian employees and a myriad of federal service programs, the number seems less significant when compared with the 10.8 million state and local employees and the aggregate of countless state and local agencies that maintain personal-information data files. Of equal significance, are the files in the private sector, concerning such personal matters as health, insurance, credit and financing, memberships, subscriptions, housing, etc.

Though state, local, and private systems may be overwhelming, the initial focus of the committee has been on the federal government; before attention is paid to state and local government and the private sector, the federal establishment should attempt to get its own house in order. Accordingly, with a few exceptions, the Privacy Committee's initial activities have affected the federal family of agencies.

The core staff of the Privacy Committee is small, with the principal manpower for Committee work being supplied by the member agencies which are: the Secretaries of the Department of the Treasury, Department of Defense, Department of Commerce, Department of Labor, and Department of Health, Education, and Welfare; the Attorney General; the chairman of the United States Civil Service Commission; the directors of the Office of Management and Budget and the Office of Telecommunications Policy; and the Special Assistant to the President for Consumer Affairs. Each of these agencies has assigned staff or task forces to work on various projects, either in a lead or contributing capacity, depending upon the nature of the effort and the interest and expertise of the particular member agency.

Planned Projects of the Committee

Here is a list of some of the projects and initiatives commenced under the auspices of the committee:

1. Development of standards for computer system and network security. This initiative should have benefits for all levels of government and the private sector, for it contemplates the development of personal-information categories in terms of confidentiality requirements, together with standards to safeguard systems containing personal information.

2. Recommendations for legislation that will:

☐ Provide confidentiality and security requirements for federal data banks

☐ Establish confidentiality and security requirement for criminal justice information systems

☐ Provide increased confidentiality for tax information

☐ Establish federal practices in preemployment personnel background investigations

Though these activities are directed mainly at the federal level, hopefully our experience will provide useful guidance to other levels of government, and to the private sector, as they assume roles in programs to ensure the confidentiality of personal information.

In addition to what may be gained through "spillover" from federally oriented activities, there are a few studies and programs that have broader impact:

☐ A survey of private sector preemployment practices as regards personnel background investigations

☐ The development of a consumer code of fair information practices that can be voluntarily subscribed to by business and industry

☐ Examination of the Fair Credit Reporting Act to develop recommendations for improving legislative safeguards on behalf of the consumer

☐ Support for legislation establishing stronger privacy protections for access to customer financial records maintained by banks

☐ Support of legislation, which has now been enacted, to protect the confidentiality of student records maintained by schools, colleges and universities, and to provide for access to records by students and parents

As is obvious from these opening efforts of the Privacy Committee, the scope of the mandate is broad, and there is much yet to be done as a program is shaped.

In December [1974], a symposium with representatives of state and local government considered a strategy for governmental cooperation in developing and implementing privacy and confidentiality safeguards; the report of that session soon will be available. Consistent with the concepts of the "New Federalism," governmental partnership in program development is being pursued in privacy initiatives, as well as other government service programs.

We also look to cooperative efforts with the private sector in developing responsible practices with regard to the handling of personal information about clients and consumers.

The present goal of the committee is to develop a "self-executive program"—one that develops an awareness and acceptance by *all* people.

Even without evil intent, inadequate regard for the practices surrounding the use and maintenance of information can result in the violation of individual privacy.

Next, we look to the development of fair information practices, consistent with the principles mentioned earlier in this article, that can be adopted by government and the private sector.

The operations of government and business should not be couched in the maintenance of personal information hidden from the data subjects and unverified by objective standards of accuracy and reliability. Surely there has not been enough attention paid to these considerations in the past, and the work of the Privacy Committee is bringing to light some of those failures.

Nothing can be more sacred to our democratic society than the security of the citizen in his home, and the privacy of the individual in the conduct of his personal affairs. The Privacy Committee is working to that end, and if all citizens, government, and businesses join the effort, the objective can be achieved.

PRIVACY AND SOCIETY [3]

The issue of the right to privacy is at a crossroads. The policy choices to be made in the next few years will determine whether our nation will leash technology to prevent its stampede over the right to privacy, or whether enormous interconnected data systems carrying information about all of us will grow unchecked.

Until recently, the available technology made difficult the automatic transfer of information gathered by one agency for one purpose to another agency for another purpose without the knowledge of the individual.

Suddenly, Americans have become intensely aware that the situation has changed. Now they are faced with an erosion of their privacy, for which they will receive no benefit or right in exchange. In fact, the entire process of collection

[3] From article by Henry M. Jackson, United States Senator (Democrat, Washington), chairman of the Committee on Interior and Insular Affairs. *Humanist.* 35:30-2. My./Je. '75. This article first appeared in *The Humanist* May/June 1975 issue and is reprinted by permission.

and transfer of information can and does occur without the individual's knowledge, let alone his or her consent. What is lost, as much as the right to privacy, is the right to control one's life.

By living in a diffuse society, certain rights to privacy are automatically surrendered by everyone. No one has, or should have, the right to keep his or her income private from the Internal Revenue Service. That is one cost of living in a democracy. There are other rights to privacy that some citizens choose to give up voluntarily. When a person wants a privilege that others do not have—whether it is a government job, a credit card, or an educational scholarship—there is an implicit understanding that the goal is important enough to warrant giving out some relevant personal information. In that case, since it is a conscious decision, made with the knowledge of how it will be used, the individual retains his or her free choice.

Recent disclosures by William E. Colby, director of the Central Intelligence Agency, confirmed that American reporters and political dissidents have been spied upon, that the mail of private citizens has been opened, that CIA agents were planted as informers inside domestic protest groups, and that CIA agents assembled secret files on over ten thousand Americans.

The Privacy Act

The Ninety-third Congress, which ended in December [1974], has been referred to as the "privacy" Congress because of the legislation it grappled with—over two hundred bills—in an attempt to regain for each person the right to privacy, the right to know what information is being kept, and thus the right to make choices about his or her life. The bills covered a wide area, including Army surveillance, government record-keeping, criminal-arrest records, federal employees' polygraphs, the Census, financial records, mailing lists, freedom of information, Social Security numbers, a privacy commission, income tax returns, and telephone communications.

One of the most monumental of these bills, the Privacy Act of 1974, which I cosponsored, became law on December 31, 1974. This law gives individuals, for the first time, the right to know they are the subjects of a file, to examine its contents, to challenge its contents, and to correct inaccurate, incomplete, or out-of-date information.

Moreover, the Privacy Act forces government agencies to ensure that the information they keep on individuals is accurate and relevant and to make public how the information in government data banks and information systems is routinely used. The act specifically excludes gathering of information about the political or religious beliefs of any person, unless authorized by law, and requires the written consent of the individual before any information is used in other than a routine way.

The original Senate privacy bill would have created a privacy-protection commission to implement the Privacy Act. The final version that passed substituted a study commission for the original proposal. This seven-member commission will sit for two years and will gather information on government and private data banks to form the basis for future legislation. Authority for implementing the act was given to the Office of Management and Budget.

This landmark Privacy Act, which passed Congress on December 18, also recognized the dangers of permitting the Social Security number to become a universal identifier. It banned any new government activity from making any right, benefit, or privilege conditional upon disclosure of a Social Security number. Systems in effect before January 1, 1975, that have relied upon the Social Security number, can continue. But from now on, a person who is asked to give his or her Social Security number must be told the nature and authority and purpose of the request and, if he or she decides not to give it, may not be denied the right in question unless disclosure is expressly provided for by law.

In my mind, there was no doubt of the need for the Privacy Act. A lengthy report issued by former Senator Sam Ervin's Subcommittee on Constitutional Rights of the Senate Judiciary Committee indicated that as of 1970, fifty-four federal agencies would admit to keeping 858 data banks containing over 1.25 billion records on individuals. The committee stated emphatically in its report that it was under no illusion that all of the existing data banks had been reported. The report concluded, "The varying degrees of thoroughness and candor displayed by the fifty-four agencies surveyed showed dramatically the need for legislation to overcome this apparent reluctance on the part of federal agencies to disclose to the Congress and the people the nature and scope of their data banks."

The 858 data banks fell into three categories, according to the report. Sixty-nine percent were mainly administrative; that is, they were created to help agencies administer programs. About 15 percent were evaluative; that is, they contained information used to make decisions on the status of individuals. Sixteen percent were statistical; that is, they collected information about groups of subjects for management and planning. At least 29 of the 858 were created to collect derogatory information about people. Three fourths of these files were computerized.

When asked about the authority that enabled the agencies to create these data banks, 84 percent of the 844 data banks responding could not cite explicit statutory authority, and 18 percent could cite no statutory authority at all. There were 16 percent with express statutory authority, 21 percent with derivative statutory authority, and 45 percent with implied statutory authority, a weaker justification. These facts are very important. They show that some agencies have set up information systems that have the potential to invade our collective privacy without any authority whatsoever and that others rest on very shaky statutory ground.

Oversight Committee

Landmark though the Privacy Act was, it left untouched other areas affecting privacy that are of equal concern.

Congress must safeguard privacy rights with an unprecedented vigilance. It can do so only if it continually reviews the government's surveillance activities and determines whether any changes are needed in the law or the governmental structure to protect an individual's privacy against unlawful or even unwarranted intrusions. It was to this end that Senator Gaylord Nelson of Wisconsin and I proposed a joint congressional committee to oversee the activities of all government agencies with investigative or surveillance powers.

This committee would continually review government agencies conducting surveillance to determine if the protection of individual liberties, and especially the individual's right to privacy, requires any changes in the law or the governmental structure. It would examine the nature and scope of agencies' surveillance activities. At least once a year, officials from these agencies would appear before the committee with documents and other evidence and give sworn testimony about their surveillance activities. The committee would have the power to subpoena other individuals, private or public, to testify or give evidence about the government's surveillance actions.

Currently, Congress has no way to discover the nature and scope of government surveillance. Government investigating and surveillance has got out of hand partly because there is no central overseeing committee. At least twelve House and Senate committees now share overseeing responsibility over all federal agencies that conduct investigative activities. While overseeing agency performance may not be the most glamorous job, I feel strongly that this committee is needed as a permanent focal point, so that Congress can retain control over our constitutional rights.

Besides its overseeing function, the committee also would

review the sharing of information practices among federal agencies and similar local and state agencies. Due to the proliferation in recent years of computerized data banks linked by high-speed communications, this is particularly important. The committee would focus on what, if any, changes are needed in those intergovernmental relationships to protect individual liberties and would decide whether needed changes can best be effected through reorganization of federal agencies or enactment of laws.

The need for this legislation is beyond dispute. In 1967, it was estimated that over 50 federal agencies were engaged in investigative actions, employing over 20,000 investigators. Both the number of agencies and the number of investigators have certainly grown since then, and it is now very clear that the investigative powers of the federal government have been carelessly and on occasion willfully abused for illegitimate purposes. This obviously represents a threat to the integrity of individual rights and to our entire way of life. Through this joint committee, we would try to reverse an unfortunate government attitude that seems willing to tolerate violations of individual privacy in the pursuit of information it deems useful.

Wiretap Investigation

There is another area about which I am deeply concerned, and that is the whole spectrum of wiretapping, eavesdropping, and electronic surveillance. The Permanent Subcommittee on Investigations, which I chair, has been collecting data from numerous federal agencies on these subjects.

This information, once compiled, will likely be used as the basis for legislation dealing with these subjects. A detailed questionnaire was sent out early . . . [in 1974] asking scores of government departments and independent agencies about their surveillance policies and activities, including use of personnel and equipment. Although it has been difficult and time-consuming getting replies, we feel this questionnaire is a very important start toward identifying, isolating, and eliminating all unwarranted government surveillance. The civil liberties of all our citizens are at stake. History has shown us, the Watergate scandals have shown us, that the executive branch alone cannot impose the controls required to protect each citizen's constitutional rights. Yet with inadequate controls, and with no checks, it is possible that we could all be victims of surveillance technology.

However, let me emphasize that it is not my intent to cripple the fight against organized or unorganized crime, nor is it my intent to allow those engaged in espionage to conduct their nefarious activities with impunity. With a balanced approach, we can continue to fight crime and the loss of its privacy. We must move ahead on both fronts without substituting one right for another.

So far, our investigation has shown questionable practices by the government and disturbing situations of improper wiretapping and eavesdropping in the private sector, from allegations of company takeovers, illegal manufacture of equipment, and eavesdropping on organized labor, to the possibility of spying in professional sports.

Conclusion

The headstrong spirit characteristic of this nation has given us a peculiar history of single-minded pursuit of technological advances without studying the repercussions of such advances until much later in the game.

We are now much later in the game. Having used and refined and often benefited and sometimes suffered from our technology, we have reached a watershed in the protection of our right to privacy.

One of the foremost privacy experts, Alan F. Westin, has warned that delaying solid policy decisions any longer may price privacy out of the market.

The Ninety-third Congress, in passing the Privacy Act, delved seriously into these issues. The Ninety-fourth Congress, I pledge, will continue in that fashion so that it will

be said of our era that we made our privacy safe from
technology.

ON CURBING WIRETAPPING [4]

The time has come for Congress to end the wiretapping
abuses perpetrated in the name of national security. The
need for legislation is clear. National security taps are not
authorized by a judicial warrant. The government alone is
free to determine whom it can tap and when it can tap.

Warrantless taps pose a grave danger to fundamental
constitutional liberties. Generally they are not supported
by concrete evidence to justify the invasion of an individual's privacy. And always they escape the scrutiny of the
courts, the Congress, and the public at large because the
government is not required to disclose their existence unless
it prosecutes the individual involved—a rare occurrence in
the history of national security wiretaps.

The danger of warrantless wiretaps is not confined to
the truly criminal and subversive element within our society.
Warrantless wiretaps are a serious threat to everyone, regardless of his or her station in life.

The list of those who have been wiretapped includes
many illustrious names: Martin Luther King Jr., Joseph
Kraft, a number of newspaper reporters, government officials, congressional aides, and friends of White House staff
members.

These cases demonstrate that often these taps are employed to ensure the political security of the Administration
and not the security of the nation. They also demonstrate
the wisdom of the Fourth Amendment's protection.

[4] From "Warrantless Bugs: The Invisible Pests," by Gaylord Nelson, United
States Senator (Democrat, Wisconsin). *Trial.* 11:64-5+. Mr./Ap. '75. Reprinted
by permission of *Trial* magazine, © 1975, published bi-monthly by The Association of Trial Lawyers of America. All rights reserved.

Fourth Amendment Protection

The Fourth Amendment was intended to protect each citizen from unreasonable invasion of privacy. It guarantees that privacy can be invaded only when there is a judicial warrant based on probable cause.

Of course, our Founding Fathers did not contemplate the advent of telecommunications. The individual's right to privacy is nonetheless equally violated when the government breaks into someone's telephone conversation as when it breaks into someone's home.

In the 1967 decisions of *Berger v. New York* and *Katz v. United States,* the Supreme Court held that the Fourth Amendment generally requires the government to obtain a judicial warrant before it can wiretap.

The Court later reaffirmed this decision in *Alderman v. United States* (394 US 165 [1969]) and *United States v. United States District Court* (407 US 297 [1972]) commonly referred to as the *Keith* case. The Court stated in the *Keith* case that the government cannot use warrantless wiretaps even when the citizens' activities threatened the domestic security of the nation.

The Court has not yet ruled on whether the Fourth Amendment also applies to cases involving foreign powers and their agents. In *Keith,* the Court specifically stated it did not consider cases where citizens "have significant connection" with foreign powers and their agents.

Taps and the Executive Branch

Because the Court has not ruled on these national security matters, the government has maintained that it can still install warrantless wiretaps in certain situations. In a September 1973 letter to Senator William Fulbright, then chairman of the Senate Foreign Relations Committee, then Attorney General Elliot Richardson stated that the Administration would continue to install warrantless wiretaps against private individuals and domestic organizations if the Administration believed their activities affected national security.

Testifying before two Senate subcommittees . . . [in 1974] Attorney General William Saxbe said that the Administration would continue to use warrantless wiretaps in national security cases and that he opposed legislation to prohibit use of warrantless wiretaps. In explaining this position, the Attorney General said:

The sensitivity of the intelligence in these cases cannot possibly be evaluated by persons who do not regularly deal with foreign affairs and intelligence matters. The judgment requires consideration of information that cannot be available to the judiciary. . . . Put another way, the question is this: Because of some apparent abuses, should the President be denied the power to authorize a national security surveillance? . . . My answer is an emphatic No.

The Attorney General's testimony ignores the dangers involved when the justification and execution of such wiretaps are the sole province of the executive branch. There is no opportunity for the Congress, a court, or any other public body to examine the exercise of that discretion in order to prevent abuses. The problem here can be appreciated by a brief review of the governmental use of national security wiretaps.

On the eve of World War II, President Franklin D. Roosevelt became convinced that use of warrantless wiretaps would be necessary to protect the nation against the "fifth column" and other subversive elements. Roosevelt, therefore, instructed his attorney general, Robert Jackson, to authorize wiretaps against subversives and suspected spies.

He was sensitive, however, to the practical risks and constitutional dangers of wiretapping. Accordingly, he ordered the attorney general to keep them to a minimum and to "limit them insofar as possible to aliens."

Roosevelt's sensitivity to the dangers of wiretapping is indicated in a memorandum to Jackson dated May 21, 1940, in which he agreed with the Supreme Court's interpretation of section 605 of the Federal Communications Act of 1934: "Under ordinary and normal circumstances wiretapping by government agents should not be carried on for the excellent reason that it is almost bound to lead to abuse of civil rights."

The questionable legality of wiretapping did not deter its use after World War II. In the 1950s and 1960s the government's reliance on warrantless wiretaps mushroomed. The precautions taken by Roosevelt to prevent abuse were not taken, however. Indeed, the wiretap program was expanded to include many domestic criminal matters.

The use of warrantless wiretaps had become a monster with its own momentum. Even the President did not always know the full extent to which such taps were used.

And in 1965, Johnson issued a directive placing severe restrictions on the use of warrantless wiretaps. Johnson initially made clear his general opposition to warrantless taps: "I am strongly opposed to the interception of telephone conversations as a general investigative technique."

Johnson nonetheless ordered that wiretaps be permitted in national security cases where there was specific authorization from the attorney general. Johnson apparently believed in good faith that this authorization would safeguard the individual's constitutional right to privacy. Sadly, but not unexpectedly, this belief proved illusory. Examples of abuse abound.

Wiretap Abuses

In 1969 the Administration installed warrantless taps on thirteen government officials and four members of the press for the purported reason that these individuals were leaking or publishing sensitive information involving foreign governments. There was little or no concrete evidence to justify the taps, and in many cases the evidence showed that the tapped individual did not even have access to the information. In at least two cases, the taps were continued after the individual had left the government service and had joined the presidential campaign staff of Senator Muskie.

The White House authorized the burglary of the home of newspaper columnist Joseph Kraft, again on national security grounds, so that a warrantless tap could be installed. There was not, and is not, any evidence that Mr. Kraft was acquiring or reporting any information which compromised our national security.

Senate Watergate Committee testimony on the Pentagon Papers investigation shows that the White House authorized warrantless taps on numerous individuals, including congressional aides whose only relationship with the case was friendship with reporters covering it.

In 1970 the White House conceived and drafted a broad plan for warrantless wiretaps, burglary, and other insidious surveillance practices. The staff assistant responsible for the plan stated in a memorandum to the President that certain aspects were "clearly illegal," yet the plan was approved. It was only scrapped later, when J. Edgar Hoover objected.

And . . . the CIA [has] confirmed newspaper reports that it . . . used warrantless taps in the 1960s to spy on the activities of American citizens whose principle "crime" was to criticize government policies.

Greater protection against warrantless wiretapping is obviously needed. The government cannot make a disinterested judgment as to whether a planned search by government agents is reasonable. The government cannot properly be both advocate and judge of its own conduct.

This essential point was made by Justice Douglas in the *Katz* case:

Neither the President nor the Attorney General is a magistrate. . . . Under the separation of powers created by the Constitution, the executive branch is not supposed to be neutral and disinterested. Rather, it should vigorously investigate and prevent breaches of national security and prosecute those who violate the pertinent federal laws. . . . Since spies and saboteurs are as entitled to that protection of the Fourth Amendment as suspected gamblers . . . I cannot agree that where spies and saboteurs are involved adequate protection of Fourth Amendment rights is assured when the President and attorney general assume both the positions of adversary—and prosecutor—and disinterested, neutral magistrate.

In short, regardless of how beneficent the government's intentions, warrantless wiretaps pose serious danger to constitutional rights and liberties.

Time for Change

Whatever the rationale for past inaction, it is clear that Congress must act now to insure the preservation of precious constitutional rights—especially the right to privacy. Invocation of "national security" cases should not enable the government to wiretap without regard to traditional constitutional limitations.

I am presently proposing a bill which would prohibit the use of warrantless wiretaps for national security reasons or any other purpose. Among other provisions, this bill includes the following changes:

☐ Before the government could wiretap American citizens in national security cases it would have to obtain a judicial warrant based on probable cause that a crime had been, or was about to be, committed. This change would merely be a reaffirmation of the individual's rights under the Fourth Amendment, which requires all government searches—including wiretaps—to have the prior approval of a judicial warrant based on probable cause.

☐ Before the government could wiretap a foreign agent it would have to obtain a judicial warrant based on information that the wiretap is necessary for national security reasons. This provision would not in any way undermine the government's ability to protect against foreign attack or subversion. Judges will be most responsive to government requests any time there is a real need to wiretap. And experience with domestic wiretaps shows that judges will jealously guard sensitive information made available to them.

☐ Within thirty days after the last authorized interception of American citizens, the government would have to
disclose the existence of the taps to those under surveillance.
This disclosure could be delayed if the government satisfies
the court that the individual is engaged in a continuing
criminal enterprise or that disclosure would endanger national security interests.

In most cases, this change would enable the individual
tapped to seek judicial relief for any violations of his rights.

The courts could guard the right to privacy in one of
two ways. Either they could refuse to issue a warrant authorizing a government search, or they could respond to an
individual's complaint that the government had conducted
an unconstitutional search. In the present situation there
is usually no way for the individuals to know that their
calls are being intercepted.

For decades the government has used warrantless wiretaps to serve its view of the national security. These wiretaps have always posed a fundamental danger to the freedoms guaranteed by the Constitution. The Watergate scandals have dramatically demonstrated the danger in our
midst. The right to privacy, as well as the other constitutional liberties are the cornerstone of our democratic system.
If those rights and liberties are eroded, the very fabric of
our constitutional system is imperiled. Congress should
therefore act now to protect our cherished rights and liberties from abusive national security wiretaps.

CITIZENS' LOOK AT PRIVACY [5]

Privacy in a free society has suddenly come alive—an
issue that must be reckoned with if we are to preserve one
of the fundamental rights of our democracy. . . .

[5] Synopsis of the findings of the Roscoe Pound-American Trial Lawyers
Foundation conference on "privacy in a free society," prepared by Richard S.
Jacobson, editor of *Trial* magazine. In "A Massive Blow on the Anvil of
Privacy," by Richard S. Jacobson. *Trial.* 11:14-15. Ja./F. '75. Reprinted by per-
mission of *Trial* magazine, © 1974, published bi-monthly by The Association of
Trial Lawyers of America. All rights reserved.

Thus, privacy in our free society—the conflict during the last decade and a half over the rights of the citizens and the rights of government and business—becomes a vocal issue.

Watergate, in demonstrating how the invasion of citizens' privacy became a threat to our democratic free society, gives Samson-like strength to the vocal action.

Herbert H. Bennett of Portland, Maine, president of the Roscoe Pound–American Trial Lawyers Foundation, one of America's most prestigious legal research organizations and one of the first groups to take an in-depth look at the conflict and the problems, said: "It was only last June when the New York *Times* [June 1974] editorialized at the 'ineffectual alarm' over the growing cancer of invasion of privacy":

The American capacity to collect and store information about individuals and the American tendency to express ineffectual alarm at the development have grown enormously in the last decade and a half . . . [and] the nation is left with a vague sense that the information monsters inevitably threaten to transform the society in which we live. . . .

According to Bennett . . . [the apprehension expressed by Max Lerner, professor of political science and columnist], "Of the many things we have done to Democracy in the past, the worst has been the indignity of taking it for granted," prompted the Foundation to make "privacy in a free society" the theme of its 1974 Annual Chief Justice Earl Warren Conference on Advocacy.

Conference Chairman T. I. Koskoff of Bridgeport, Connecticut, selected three of the nation's outstanding professors and activists on electronic surveillance, political informing tactics, and data banks and dossiers to prepare in-depth "background papers" on these privacy issues.

Then, a citizens' group of fifty of America's most learned and talented men and women in this field were invited to study the "background papers" in light of their own knowledge. Later (June, 1974), they attended a plenary conference to evolve a consensus of findings to provide a base for affirmative legislative action.

The conferees in their final report revealed sensational findings—findings which showed remarkable unanimity on the subject, yet emphasized the independently provocative thinking of these capable individuals.

Essence of the Report

In essence, the Foundation's report called for:

☐ A ban on bugging of American citizens;

☐ Abandonment of present federal government activities in political surveillance;

☐ Restricting and redesigning all data and citizen dossier handling systems;

☐ Abolishment of the universal practice of Social Security card disclosure; and

☐ Creation of a fair information practice code.

Unable to participate in the Conference because of illness, but agreeing with 75 to 80 percent of the report's background papers, William C. Sullivan, former No. 3 man in the FBI and a thirty-year veteran, wrote a devastating letter with recommendations for FBI changes to protect privacy, internal national security and intelligence gathering activities.

The letter and recommendations—while not a part of the Foundation conferees' findings—were contained in the report.

Writing that "the need for government to control itself is certainly germane to the theme of the Conference [and that] it is remarkably timely when put within the context of the Watergate Affair," Sullivan called for:

☐ Dismantling the FBI's present responsibility for internal security and intelligence

☐ Transferring the responsibility to a newly created independent board of citizens acting as a buffer between Congress and the White House

□ Initiating a study by scholars, with ample public hearings in various sections of the country, to define, for the first time, internal and domestic security and intelligence. . . .

Explaining why the Foundation sought interdisciplinary critical examination of the subject from such a diverse group as computer scientists, law enforcement officials, law professors, lawyers, businessmen, congressmen, journalists, political scientists and philosophers, Bennett and Koskoff said:

We are in a crisis of reason. Even after two years of Watergate's lessons we have not begun to understand the implications of Democracy. . . . For the sake of the future, we must be held accountable. We must respond.

Both technology, with its surging seemingly uncontrollable momentum, and the arrogance of ambitious politicians threaten the vitality of individual rights. But the fault does not lie entirely with men of technology or self-serving politicians. It lies with us.

The Foundation's report came at the height of an "aura of fear and distrust" in our society, the expansion of all aspects of political informing and interference with citizens' First Amendment rights. . . .

A synopsis of the Conference's complete findings follows.

On Electronic Surveillance

□ No electronic surveillance for domestic intelligence. (Adopted by substantial majority.) . . .

□ No electronic surveillance for law enforcement. (Adopted by a narrow margin.)

(While there was general skepticism regarding the effectiveness of electronic surveillance, a narrow majority believed that law enforcement officials should not be allowed to use it even for crime detection. A minority believed electronic surveillance should remain available but used for only very serious crimes and under very strict control.)

□ State and local authorities should not be allowed to engage in electronic surveillance. (Vote evenly divided.)

(A sharp split developed over whether state and local law enforcement officials really need electronic surveillance, whether they have used it excessively and indiscriminately, and whether judicial and other controls in the statute do and can function properly on the state level.)

☐ No electronic surveillance should be carried out without a court order for any purpose on American citizens on US soil or on American citizens in foreign countries. (Adopted overwhelmingly.)

☐ To the extent that electronic surveillance is permitted for law enforcement, it should be limited to crimes of the utmost gravity. (Adopted by a large majority.)

(The conference reached no final definition of "crimes of utmost gravity" except that they certainly include imminent threat to life.)

☐ If used at all, electronic surveillance for law enforcement should be permitted only by court order and on probable cause subject to strict restraints. (Adopted overwhelmingly.)

☐ No bugging of any room. (Adopted by large majority.)

(Bugging was seen as a more insidious invasion of privacy than telephone tapping.)

☐ If any federal electronic surveillance is permitted, the authority should be limited to a single governmental agency —the United States Justice Department. (Adopted overwhelmingly.)

☐ The precise procedures and criteria for eavesdropping authorized by the Justice Department should be made aware to the citizenry at public hearings in various parts of the country. (Adopted overwhelmingly.)

☐ A very strong congressional oversight committee should be established to review all federal wiretaps. (Adopted unanimously.)

☐ A reporting system should be undertaken by the Justice Department subject to proper regulations to maintain confidentiality, so that all information disclosed by taps can be given to the congressional oversight committee. (Adopted unanimously.)

□ A specific minimum amount of damages should be available for any violation of wiretapping statutes by federal, state or local officials. (Adopted overwhelmingly.)

On Political Informing

(The conferees differentiated between informing for political reasons or motives and informing on political activities. Informing for political reasons "should not be condoned under any circumstances.")

□ Every government agency should be barred from collecting any data concerning political activity, association or expression—protected under the First Amendment—and should destroy any such data now in existence. (Adopted overwhelmingly.)

□ An informant should not be used for surreptitious surveillance except on court order based on probable cause and subject to the same restraints as electronic surveillance. (Adopted overwhelmingly.)

□ An independent executive agency should be established with authority to insure compliance with the two above-mentioned recommendations and to receive and to act on citizens' complaints. (Very narrowly defeated.)

On Data Banks and Civilian Dossiers

□ Every public and private organization which processes personal information should be bound by the following (five) principles:

1. The data collector should owe every data subject a legally recognized fiduciary duty of reasonable care and fair dealing.

2. The data collector should collect only that information which is demonstrably necessary and relevant to a proper purpose of the organization.

3. The data collector should provide adequate systems for data security including technical administrative and personnel safeguards.

4. The data collector should provide the data subject

with a right of access to his own files, plus procedures for challenging and correcting erroneous or irrelevant information.

5. The data collector should destroy or seal all obsolete information.

(All five principles were adopted by nearly unanimous vote.)

☐ Enactment of a federal code of fair information practices, which would closely regulate the collection, storage, dissemination and use of personal information. (Adopted by nearly unanimous vote.)

☐ Collection of data by single individuals for essentially personal purposes should be exempt from any legislation. (Adopted by unanimous vote.)

☐ Data subjects should be given the right of legal action for violations of the fair information practices code, and the code should be implemented and enforced by a federal agency. (Adopted by nearly unanimous vote.)

☐ No person should be compelled to divulge his Social Security number, unless expressly required to do so by law. (Adopted by nearly unanimous vote.)

BIBLIOGRAPHY

An asterisk (*) preceding a reference indicates that the article or a part of it has been reprinted in this book.

BOOKS, PAMPHLETS, AND DOCUMENTS

Adams, Paul and others. Children's rights. Praeger. '71.

Bogan, E. C. and others. The rights of gay people; an American Civil Liberties handbook. Avon. '75.

Breckenridge, A. C. The right to privacy. University of Nebraska Press. '70.

Chief Justice Earl Warren Conference on Advocacy in the United States, 1974. Privacy in a free society; final report. Roscoe Pound-American Trial Lawyers Foundation. 20 Garden St. Cambridge, Mass. 02138. '74.
Synopsis of findings, prepared by Richard S. Jacobson, *In* Trial. 11:14-15. Ja./F. '75. A massive blow on the anvil of privacy.

Columbia Human Rights Law Review staff, eds. Surveillance, data-veillance and personal freedom; a symposium. Burdick. '74.

Cowan, Paul and others. State secrets: police surveillance in America. Holt. '74.

Dorsen, Norman. Frontiers of civil liberties. Pantheon. '68.

Dorsen, Norman and Gillers, Stephen, eds. None of your business: government secrecy in America. Viking. '74.

Fraenkel, O. K. The rights we have. Crowell. '71.

Fraenkel, O. K. The rights you have. Warner Paperback Library. '72.

Friedman, Leon, ed. The civil rights reader; basic documents of the civil rights movement. Walker. '67.

Garrison, O. V. Spy government; the emerging police state in America. Lyle Stuart. '67.

Hoffman, L. J. Security and privacy in computer systems. Melville. '73.

Levine, A. H. and others. The rights of students; the basic ACLU guide to a student's rights. Dutton. '73.

Long, E. V. The intruders: the invasion of privacy by government and industry. Praeger. '67.

Lowi, T. J. ed. Private life and public order; the context of modern public policy. Norton. '68.

McClellan, G. S. ed. Civil rights. (Reference Shelf, v 36 no 6) Wilson. '64.

Miller, A. R. The assault on privacy. University of Michigan Press. '71.

*Neier, Aryeh. Dossier: the secret files they keep on you. Stein and Day. '75.

Pember, D. R. Privacy and the press; the law, the mass media, and the First Amendment. University of Washington Press. '72.

Raines, J. C. Attack on privacy. Judson Press. '74.

Rioux, J. W. and Sandow, S. A. eds. Children, parents, and school records. National Committee for Citizens in Education. Columbia, Md. 21043. '74.

Rule, J. B. Private lives and public surveillance; social control in the computer age. Schocken. '74.

Scheingold, S. A. The politics of rights; lawyers, public policy, and political change. Yale University Press. '74.

Severn, William. The right to privacy. Washburn. '73.

Sigler, J. A. American rights policies. Dorsey. '75.

Tresolini, R. J. These liberties; case studies in civil rights. Lippincott. '68.

United States. Congress. House. Committee on Banking, Housing and Urban Affairs. Subcommittee on Financial Institutions. Amend the Bank secrecy act: hearings, August 11 and 14, 1972. . . . 92d Congress, 2d Session. The Committee. Washington, D.C. 20510. '72.

United States. Congress. House. Committee on Government Operations. Subcommittee on Foreign Operations and Government Information. Records maintained by government agencies: hearings, June 22 and 27, 1972. . . . 92d Congress, 2d Session. The Committee. Washington, D.C. 20515. '72.

United States. Congress. House. Committee on Post Office and Civil Service. Subcommittee on Postal Operations. Mailing lists: hearings, July 22 and 23, 1970. . . . 91st Congress, 2d Session. The Committee. Washington, D.C. 20515. '70.

United States. Congress. Senate. Committee on the Judiciary. Subcommittee on Constitutional Rights. Army surveillance of civilians: a documentary analysis. 92d Congress, 2d Session. Supt. of Docs. Washington, D.C. 20402. '72.

United States. Congress. Senate. Committee on the Judiciary. Subcommittee on Constitutional Rights. Federal data banks and constitutional rights, a study of data systems on individuals maintained by agencies of the United States government, summary and conclusions. 93d Congress, 2d Session. Supt. of Docs. Washington, D.C. 20402. '74.

United States. Congress. Senate. Committee on the Judiciary. Subcommittee on Constitutional Rights. Military surveillance of civilian politics: a report. 93d Congress, 1st Session. Supt. of Docs. Washington, D.C. 20402. '73.

United States. Congress. Senate. Committee on the Judiciary. Subcommittee on Constitutional Rights. Privacy, the census and federal questionnaires: hearings: April 24-July 1, 1969. . . . 91st Congress, 1st Session. Supt. of Docs. Washington, D.C. 20402. '70.

United States. Congress. Senate. Committee on the Judiciary. Subcommittee on Constitutional Rights. Uncle Sam is watching you; highlights from the hearings; introduction by Alan Barth. Public Affairs Press. '71.

United States. Department of Health, Education, and Welfare. Records, computers, and the rights of citizens; report of Secretary's Advisory Committee on Automated Personal Data Systems. Supt. of Docs. Washington, D.C. 20402. '73.

Warner, Malcolm and Stone, M. G. The data bank society: organizations, computers and social freedom. Allen & Unwin. '70.

Westin A. F. ed. Freedom now! the civil-rights struggle in America. Basic Books. '64.

Westin, A. F. ed. Information technology in a democracy. Harvard University Press. '71.

Westin, A. F. Privacy and freedom. Atheneum. '67.
   Extensive bibliography for materials on privacy up to 1967.

Westin, A. F. and Baker, M. A. Databanks in a free society. Quadrangle. '74.

Wheeler, Stanton, ed. On record: files and dossiers in American life. Russell Sage Foundation. 230 Park Ave. New York 10017. '70.

PERIODICALS

American School Board Journal. 162:44+. Ja. '75. If the new student privacy law has you confused, perhaps that's because you're sane. M. H. Cutler.

*Cable Report. 4:1-2. Ja. '75. I wonder who's watching me now. Jerrold Oppenheim.

Christian Century. 91:663. Je. 26, '74. Another Watergate fallout: the erosion of privacy. J. M. Wall.

*Christian Science Monitor. p F 8. Ja. 11, '74. Court's search decision: two views. Frank Carrington and L. L. Weinreb.

*Christian Science Monitor. p 26. Je. 11, '75. Extracts from the Rockefeller CIA report. R. L. Strout.

Christianity & Crisis. 32:279-82. D. 25, '72. Privacy and community: reflections on freedom in America.. J. C. Raines.

Chronicle of Higher Education. 9:8-10. Ja. 13, '75. Proposed U.S. guidelines on access to student records. U.S. Dept. of Health, Education, and Welfare. Washington, D.C. 20201.

Chronicle of Higher Education. 10:9. Mr. 31, '75. Confidentiality in psychotherapy. C. M. Fields.

Civil Liberties Review. 1:7-78. Summer '74. ℞ for surveillance; CLR special feature.

Civil Liberties Review. 1:74-8. Summer '74. Bipartisan privacy. B. M. Goldwater Jr.

Civil Liberties Review. 2:15-47. Summer '75. Electronic surveillance: the national security game. Frank Donner.

Columbia Human Rights Law Review. Winter 1972 issue.
Devoted largely to the conflict between government's need for personal information and individual's need for personal privacy.

*Columbia Journalism Review. 13:10-11. Mr./Ap. '75. Secrecy, privacy, and publicity. W. H. Hornby.

Columbia Law Review. 72:693+. Ap. '72. Invasion of privacy: a clarification of concepts. Louis Lusky.

Current. No 65:17-22. N. '65. Is privacy a constitutional right?
Excerpts from Supreme Court's decision in Griswold v. Connecticut.

Department of State Bulletin. 68:425. Ap. 9, '73. Commission on conduct of foreign policy, Mr. 9, '73.

Harper's Magazine. 247:14+. N. '73. Giving the computer a conscience; FBI's National crime information center. J. T. DeWeese.

Harper's Magazine. 248:36+. Ap. '74. Privacies of life. Paul Bender.

Harper's Magazine. 250:36-9. Je. '75. Harmonica bugs, cloaks, and silver boxes: eavesdropping in post-Watergate America. George O'Toole.

Harvard Business Review. 54:62-70. Mr./Ap. '75. Personal privacy versus the corporate computer. R. C. Goldstein and R. L. Nolan.

Harvard Educational Review. 43:481-668. N. '73; 44:6-157. F. '74. The rights of children [symposium].

*Human Events. p 1+. Ja. 11. '75. Will CIA survive this anti-intelligence mania? John Ligonier, pseud.

Human Behavior. 4:56-9. O. '75. Snoopology. John Jung.

*Humanist. 35:30-2. My./Je. '75. Privacy and society. H. M. Jackson.

Idaho Law Review. 11:11-27. Fall '74. The threads of privacy: the judicial evolution of a "right to privacy" and current legislative trends. S. D. Symms and P. M. Hawks.

Intellect. 103:230-3. Ja. '75. "National security" and electronic surveillance: the need for corrective legislation. G. A. Nelson.

Labor Law Journal. 25:270-92. My. '74. The confidentiality of

personnel records: a legal and ethical view. Mordechai Mironi.
*Nation. 220:200-4. F. 22, '75. Memos to the chairmen: the issue, of course, is power. F. J. Donner.
National Observer. p 1+. N. 30, '74. Congress says yes to privacy, no to secrecy. M. R. Arnold.
*National Observer. p 8. S. 6, '75. Name droppers . . . social security numbers become identifiers. Dori Jones.
National Observer. p 22. N. 1, '75. The invisible-ink caper. Henry Gemmill.
*New Republic. 172:18-21. Mr. 8, '75. Exposing ourselves in public. T. J. Cottle.
New Republic. 172:13-17. My. 31, '75. Unchecked wiretapping. A. M. Dershowitz.
New Republic. 172:8-11+. Je. 28, '75. Led astray by the CIA. M. H. Halperin.
*New Republic. 173:12-13. Jl. 26, '75. The most secret agents. M. H. Halperin.
New York Times. p 1+. Je. 2, '75. Inquiry reveals I.R.S. master list. Eileen Shanahan.
New York Times. p 29. D. 7, '74. A new way must be found to safeguard medical privacy. Suzanne Loebl.
New York Times. p 19. D. 24, '74. The truth is needed. Tom Wicker.
New York Times. p 12. F. 19, '75. A. T. & T. aide tells House panel of wide eavesdropping by the Bell System. N. M. Horrock.
*New York Times. p 16. F. 20, '75. Electronic surveillance: scope of wiretapping and bugging an issue of rising concern. N. M. Horrock.
*New York Times. p 12. Mr. 6, '75. Privacy vs. the press: the issue remains. Martin Arnold.
New York Times. p 21. Ap. 2, '75. Judge rules citizens have right to their credit rating reports.
New York Times. p 1+. Je. 11, '75. C.I.A. panel finds "plainly unlawful" acts that improperly invaded American rights. N. M. Horrock.
New York Times. p 18+. Je. 11, '75. Summary of Rockefeller panel's C.I.A. report.
*New York Times. p 1+. O. 6, '75. F.B.I. checking of radicals went on beyond deadline. J. M. Crewdson.
New York Times. p 1+. O. 22, '75. C.I.A. "mail cover" put at 2.7 million. N. M. Horrock.
New York Times Magazine. p 16-17+. Ap. 15, '73. Marked for life: dissemination of arrest records. Aryeh Neier.
New York University Law Review. 48:670-773. O. '73. On privacy: constitutional protection for personal liberty.

New Yorker. 51:45-50+. Ap. 21, '75. A reporter at large: Anything adverse? (Credit bureaus). Thomas Whiteside.

New Yorker. 51:50-2+. N. 3, 54-6+. N. 10, 50-2+. N. 17, '75. Annals of law; the liberty of every man (Fourth Amendment). Richard Harris.

Newsweek. 84:122. D. 9, '74. Breast cancer and news overkill. Shana Alexander.

Newsweek. 85:13. Ja. 20, '75. By the numbers. A. D. Seidenbaum.

Newsweek. 85:25. F. 3, '75. Invitation to a bonfire. Meg Greenfield.

Newsweek. 85:19-22+. Je. 23, '75. Who's watching whom. D. M. Alpern and others.

Northwestern University Law Review. 69:263-301. My./Je. '74. Constitutional right of privacy: an examination.

Phi Delta Kappan. 57:20-2. S. '75. The teacher's duty to privacy: court rulings in sexual deviancy cases. K. H. Ostrander.

Philosophy & Public Affairs. 4:295-314. Summer '75. The right to privacy. J. J. Thomson.

Philosophy & Public Affairs. 4:315-22. Summer '75. Thomson on privacy. Thomas Scanlon.

Philosophy & Public Affairs. 4:323-33. Summer '75. Why privacy is important. James Rachels.

*Privacy Journal. No 5:1+. Mr. '75. Keeping your bills secret in an electronic age. Paul Armer.

*Privacy Journal. No 9:1+. Jl. '75. The wired nation: wiretaps. R. E. Smith.

*Privacy Report. No 8:1+. Mr. '74. Do Americans really value privacy? A. S. Miller.

*Privacy Report. No 10:7-8. My. '74. Privacy is not solitude. B. L. Kaiser.

*Privacy Report. 2:1-9. F. '75. Student records: your rights under the Buckley act. T. R. Hayden.

Progressive. 38:37-9. O. '74. Kids in the computer. Hannah Shields and Mae Churchill.

Psychology Today. 8:19+. D. '74. Our despotic laws destroy the right to self-control. T. S. Szasz.

Psychology Today. 8:23+. My. '75. Privacy vs. the right to know. Pam Moore.

Public Administration Review. 32:526-30. S./O. '72. Public administrators and the "privacy thing." F. G. DeBalogh.

Reader's Digest. 105:41-2+. N. '74. What right of privacy? Irwin Ross.

The Record (Bergen County Record, Hackensack, N.J.). p 1+. Mr. 31, '75. The mailing list: invasion of privacy or a legitimate marketing tool?

*Saturday Review. 2:12-13+. Ap. 5, '75. The rise of police logic. Stephen Arons.

*Science. 188:713-15. My. 16, '75. Privacy: congressional efforts are coming to fruition. Constance Holden.

Social Problems. 21:52-64. Summer '73. Research setting and the right not to be researched. Edward Sagarin.

Social Work. 16:35-41. Ja. '71. Protecting the public's privacy in computerized health and welfare information systems. J. H. Noble Jr.

*Society. 12:7-8+. Mr./Ap. '75. Spying and security: the American way. I. L. Horowitz.

*Society. 12:62-7. S./O. '75. Computerized information and effective protection of individual rights. M. G. Bouvard and Jacques Bouvard.

Stanford Law Review. 24:550-67. F. '72. Protecting privacy in credit reporting. L. C. Garon.

State Government. 47:37-41. Winter '74. Security and privacy of criminal justice information systems. A. R. Rosenfeld.

*Trial. v 11, no 1. Ja./F. '75 issue.
   Reprinted in this book: The complexity of privacy. D. W. Metz and G. B. Trubow. p 13+; A massive blow on the anvil of privacy. R. S. Jacobson. p 14-15; The right to privacy is American. . . . M. H. Gitenstein. p 22+; But so is the right to law and order. C. M. Kelley. p 23+.

*Trial. 11:64-5+. Mr./Ap. '75. Warrantless bugs: the invisible pests. Gaylord Nelson.

U.S. News & World Report. 75:54-5. Ag. 27, '73. A secret dossier on every American?

U.S. News & World Report. 77:16. D. 30, '74. How new privacy law protects you.

U.S. News & World Report. 78:24-7. Mr. 3, '75. A national identity card for every American? [interview with Frances G. Knight, director, Passport Office, U.S. Department of State]

U.S. News & World Report. 78:18. Mr. 31, '75. Who's chipping away at your privacy?

U.S. News & World Report. 78:32-4. Je. 9, '75. Spread of police snooping.

*U.S. News & World Report. 79:61-2. Ag. 11, '75. Who's snooping into your tax returns now?

U.S. News & World Report. 79:21-2. S. 22, '75. Government snooping—how to fight back.

Vital Speeches of the Day. 39:677-81. S. 1, '73. Justice, the Constitution, and privacy; address, June 28, 1973. S. J. Ervin Jr.

Wall Street Journal. p 1+. Ag. 28, '73. Open letters: surveillance of mail by investigators raises the question of abuse. Les Gapay.

Wall Street Journal. p 20. N. 13, '74. The continuing problem of
    privacy. A. J. Large.
*Wall Street Journal. p 8. Jl. 2, '75. What about the CIA? Arthur
    Schlesinger Jr.
*Wall Street Journal. p 10. S. 4, '75. No more tiptoeing. A. L.
    Otten.
*Washington Post. p C 1-2. Je. 1, '75. Eavesdroppers behind the
    doctor's door. Natalie Davis.